AWAKE KUNDALINI

LORD GANESHA AT TRINIDAD (WEST INDIES)

Published by :
Lotus Press Publishers & Distributors

AWAKE KUNDALINI

Pt. Rajnikant Upadhyaya
Pt. Gopal Sharma

Lotus PRESS

4735/22, Prakash Deep Building
Ansari Road, Darya Ganj,
New Delhi - 110002

Lotus Press : Publishers & Distributors
Unit No. 220, 2nd Floor, 4735/22, Prakash Deep Building,
Ansari Road, Darya Ganj, New Delhi- 110002
Ph.: 41325510, 98118-38000
• E-mail : lotuspress1984@gmail.com
www.lotuspress.co.in

Awake Kundalini

ISBN: 81-8382-039-5

Printed & Published by : **Lotus Press Publishers & Distributors,** New Delhi-02

PREFACE

The ancient Indian yogic discipline recognises that man is but an inseparable constituent of, and identical with, the larger and higher Self which is Omnipotent, Omnipresent and Omniscient. Only the realisation of this identity is lacking in the ordinary human being. The yogis discovered that a limitless energy lay dormant in every human being, ready to be awakened. This dormant energy they labelled as Kundalini and likened it to a serpent lying coiled at the base of the spine, with its head turned downwards. The whole yogic discipline consists of the awakening of this Kundalini through regular practice of yoga, and directing it upwards. In due course, the Kundalini moves up the spinal cord wherein potent yet subtle energy centres, called the Chakras, lie in an inactive state. Each Chakra or energy centre has specific characteristics and its activation confers specific powers on the yogi. As the successive Chakras get activated, they confer on the practitioner of yoga immense mental and spiritual energy so that eventually nothing remains impossible for him to achieve.

This book is about the subtle energy of the life force, the pure consciousness beyond mind and the ecstatic experience of spiritual awakening. It also tells of physical collapse, psychic chaos, and personality upheaval, those elements of human transformation that uproot individuals to the core. It tells the stories of people, both ancient and modern, who have discovered and integrated an experience that pushes the edges of their sanity and their divinity.

This book is meant to introduce the reader to the ancient yogic tradition of Kundalini. You are not required to be in perfect physical shape or share any particular belief system. Kundalini Yoga works for you if you can breathe and move your body. In this type of yoga, the most important thing is experience. Your experience goes right to your heart, your core. These ancient teachings are designed to give you a hands-on approach to experiencing your deepest emotions and highest consciousness. By approaching Kundalini Yoga with openness and respect, and by following the steps included in this book, you can change and enrich your life.

This book gives you ample knowledge and guidance regarding the activation of dormant energy; but we like to warn the readers that without controlling your senses, practising proper yogic asanas, to activate kundalini is a dangerous act. Apart from the Knowledge you are going to acquire from this book, the proper guidance of a competent teacher is always recommended.

Authors

ACKNOWLEDGEMENTS

Besides all the ancient and modern scholars our deep gratitude and sincere thanks are due to Justice S. N. Kapoor and Dr. Prof. Shukdev Chaturvedi who have enlightened us with their knowledge and experience. Their moral support and cooperation was extremely valuable to us in preparation of this book.

Our friends, admirers, clients, readers and innumerable increasing letters also helped us in compiling this book for which we are grateful to all of them.

We are thankful to Shri Vind Goel, and Er. Nidhi Kaushik, Senior Lecturer Maharaja Agarsen Institute of Technology; who devoted a lot of time for material research and editing, leaving aside their own work.

We are extremely grateful to Sh. Gagan Aggarwal, President Aadi Shankaracharya Vedic Education Society & Rt. O. P. Bhardwaj, Vice-Chairman Institute of Vaastu & Joyful Living for their inspiration and encouragement to present this book in its beautiful get up for the enlightened readers.

Pracharya S. R. Jaipuria *Pt. Gopal Sharma*

CONTENTS

1

INTRODUCTION TO KUNDALINI

Kundalini, a word derived from the root word Kunda which means a 'pit' or 'cavity', is commonly described as a serpent coiled at the base of the spine in the physical body or the mooladhara chakra in the pranic equivalent.

The great ancient Saints who discovered and unfolded the secrets energy of Kundalini, have suggested that before starting Kundalini-Yoga, a person should prepare himself for it, but in modern time there are people who suggests that no preparation is required for Kundalini awakening, a number of people are following them and puting themselves in a state of confusion because due to lack of basic knowledge they are unable to understand the things properly.

The phenomena of kundalini awakening is a concept derived from Tantric yoga and is part of a rich theory describing what is usually termed the "human subtle anatomy". The idea of "subtle anatomy" is that there are aspects to human anatomy that are not physical and that cannot be perceived with the physical senses. Included here are ideas of chi and prana, meridians, nadis, chakras and kundalini. Kundalini is a component of the human subtle anatomy.

According to Tantric theory, and bodies of thought derived from it, there is within the subtle body, in a region corresponding to the base of the spine, a latent "energy"—the kundalini-that, when brought into manifestation confers both enlightenment (i.e. mystical experience) and a variety of psychic powers to the aspirant.

The idea of kundalini is almost always discussed in the context of the chakra system. The chakras are revolving vortexes, depicted as flower-like in appearance, at specific locations along the spinal axis within the subtle body. For our purposes here it is enough to say that awakening of the kundalini means the progressive ascent of the kundalini through each of the chakras, heightening the activity of that chakra and conferring expanded abilities (i.e. psychic powers and states of health) associated with that chakra.

The manifestation of the kundalini is called the "awakening" of the kundalini to stress that it is latent and must be made active. The traditional means by which kundalini is awakened involve a variety of yoga exercises passed down through the centuries including specific breath exercises and purificatory rites. However, it is also known that acts such as falling or getting hit on the head may trigger spontaneous kundalini awakening, and as well, certain drugs are known to mimic aspects of the kundalini experience.

Kundalini awakening encompasses the whole gamut of personal human experience: there are alterations at physiological, sensory, emotional, cognitive and spiritual levels. The changes produced by awakened kundalini are so drastic from our usual states of consciousness that it is reasonable to say that a person undergoing awakened kundalini is experiencing an altered state of consciousness (ASC). The person is undergoing a variety of physiological alterations including sensations of shivers or tremors moving up and down the spine, displaying spontaneous motor movements in the form of dance, hand gestures, or asa—as (sitting postures practiced in Hatha yoga), experiencing spontaneous alterations in breathing, may spontaneously cry or laugh (usually unassociated with emotional reactions) and is also experiencing alterations in perception of body temperature.

At the sensory level, both audio and visual hallucinations or visions are prominent including visions of extremely beautiful and dynamically moving geometrical figures. Also, kinesthetic and somesthetic sensations (i.e. sensations of body motion and body position, respectively) may be altered such that the person perceives themself as very large or very small. Emotionally, the person is experiencing extremes of emotions: usually either pure bliss and ecstasy or extreme fear. Empathy with others is substantially enhanced. Drastic cognitive alterations also occur.

The mind and thought process accelerate greatly, the scope and depth of the thought process expand tremendously and even ordinary objects and events are perceived to have tremendous scope and consequences. Direct intuition completely supersedes ordinary logical thinking and questions that come into the mind are directly answered with clarity and conviction through heightened intuitive processes. As well, a variety of psychic powers may potentially manifest including visions of past lives, clairvoyant visions (which could be classified as visual hallucinations), and clairaudience (audio hallucinations), amongst others.

Finally, the supreme manifestation of kundalini awakening, and the formal and proper goal of the practices leading to kundalini awakening, is the experience of enlightenment, also called satori, cosmic consciousness, or the mystical experience. Enlightenment is a direct apprehension of the unity of the cosmos, a direct apprehension and identification with the transcendental essence of life and consciousness. Its essence is a "direct knowing" and a clear comprehension into "the scheme of things". Enlightenment has been an aspect of Eastern religious thought since the beginning of known history and plays as central a role in Tantric theory as it does in any other aspect of Eastern thought.

It is clear that the awakening of the kundalini is not a series of a few small alterations in consciousness, but involves a global transformation of the entire person. The resulting state may be properly called one of hyper-awareness. As such, the fact that the kundalini experience exists at all indicates that we are dealing with an emergent property, or quality of consciousness, that results from a hyper-activation of all the systems of the body and mind. This is not a state familiar to most people. It is not even a state familiar to most people who practice kundalini yoga.

We are thus dealing with an altered state of consciousness that occurs relatively infrequently. The implication here is that, if indeed the kundalini experience is a hyperactive state of awareness, then we cannot rightly judge it by criteria used to ascertain our normal and usual states of awareness. In other words, to attempt to understand the kundalini experience, we are forced to go beyond our ordinary notions of consciousness and human nature. If we do not, then we miss the most significant aspects of the kundalini phenomena.

It should be explicitly stated that the stages leading up to kundalini awakening, as well as the experience itself, may potentially be very painful and even harmful to the individual. All texts on kundalini yoga warn of these dangers. The purificatory rites and practices are considered an essential aspect of kundalini yoga and cannot be lightly dismissed. The logic of Tantra is that the body, emotions and mind must be properly purified before attempting to awaken the kundalini, for if not, the unpurified body and mind of the person present obstacles to the kundalini itself when it is awakened.

The kundalini however will "burn" through these obstacles if present and cause severe pain to the individual at either physical, emotional or cognitive levels. Thus, as enticing as the kundalini experience may sound, it is not something one can casually seek out unless the necessary preparation is undertaken, or unless one decides beforehand to be prepared to suffer the consequences that may come with attempting to tap into the kundalini. In all of these cases, the circumstance is cathartic and related to the kundalini burning away unnecessary residues from consciousness. Though painful, such experiences in the long run are highly therapeutic.

Now, certain Western thinkers, most notably Carl Jung, have looked to these ideas of subtle anatomy, including kundalini, as aspects of the unconscious mind, and as symbolic representations of aspects of the human psyche.

1.1. HISTRICAL KNOWLEDGE

The word Kundalini is derived from a Sanskrit word 'Kundal' meaning coiled up. It is the primordial dormant energy present in three-and-a-half, coils at the base of the spine in a triangular bone called the Sacrum. The Latin name 'Os Sacrum' suggests that it is a holy or sacred part of the body. The ancient Greeks were aware of this and therefore they called it the 'Hieron Osteon', noting that it was the last bone to be destroyed when the body is burnt, and also attributed supernatural powers to it. Egyptians also held this bone to be very valuable and considered it the seat of special power.

In the West, Sacrum is symbolised by the sign of Aquarius and by the Holy Grail, container of the water of life.

The Kundalini, which is to nourish the tree of life within us, is coiled up like a serpent and therefore it has been called, 'The Serpent Power'. It has been described in great detail in the Upanishads. Kundalini Yoga is supposed to be supreme in all the Yogas. Guru Vashistha asserted that Kundalini is the seat of absolute knowledge. The awareness of the presence of this primordial energy Kundalini within the human body was considered by the sages and saints to be the highest knowledge. The Kundalini and Chakras have been vividly described in Vedic and Tantric texts.

1.1.1. Adi Sankaracharya

He lived in the 7th-8th century AD. and wrote:

> 'Having filled the pathway of the Nadis with the streaming shower of nectar flowing from the Lotus feet, having resumed thine own position from out of the resplendent Lunar regions and Thyself assuming the form of a serpent of three and a half coils, sleepest thou, in the hollow of Kula Kunda (Kula Kunda means the hollow of Mooladhara Sacrum bone)'.
>
> 'Saundarya Lahari': 'Thou art residing in secrecy with Thy Lord (The spirit) in the thousand petalled Lotus, having pierced through the Earth situated in 'Mooladhara', the Water in Manipura, the Fire abiding in the Svadhisthana, the Air in the Heart ('Anahata'), the Ether above (Visshuddhi) and 'Manas' between the eyebrows ('Agnya') and thus broken through the entire 'Kula Path'.

1.1.2. Gyaneshwara

Gyaneshwara, another famous saint of Maharashtra born around 1275 AD, described Kundalini in the 6th chapter of his famous book 'Gyaneshwari'. He wrote:

> 'Kundalini is one of the greatest energies. The whole body of the seeker starts glowing because of the rising of the Kundalini. Because of that, unwanted impurities in the body disappear. The body of the seeker suddenly looks very proportionate and the eyes look bright and attractive and the eyeballs glow.'

1.1.3. Guru Nanak Dev

Guru Nanak Dev born in 1496 AD, has made references to Kundalini awakening as mentioned below:

> "A pure heart is the golden vessel to fill the Divine Nectar which is to be sucked from the 'Dasham Dwar' through the two channels 'Ida' and 'Pingala'." Dasham Dwar means Brahmarandhra.
>
> 'God has made this human body a house with six Chakras and has established the light of spirit in it. Cross the ocean of Maya and meet the eternal God who does not come, who does not go, who neither takes birth nor dies. When your six Chakras meet in line, Surati (Kundalini) takes you beyond distortions.'

1.1.4. Holy Koran

Prophet Mohammed Sahib talked of the day of resurrection when he says that the 'hands will speak'. 'That day, we set a seal on their mouths, but their hands will speak to us, and their hands bear witness to all that they did.' When Kundalini awakening occurs, a flow of energy in the form of cool vibrations from the hands is experienced, and the various Chakras can be felt on parts of the hand and fingers.

1.1.5. Christians

Christians called it a reflection of the Holy Ghost, and worshipped its manifestations as tongues of flames over the heads of apostles during the Pentecost reunion.

Moses saw it in the form of the burning bush. During the exodus the israelites lost faith and were smitten by fiery serpents so God told Moses "make thee a serpent, and set it upon a pole: and it shall come to pass, that everyone that is bitten, when he looketh upon it, shall live. And Moses made a serpent of brass, and put it on a pole, and it came to pass, that if a fiery serpent had bitten any man, when he beheld the serpent of brass, he lived" An apt description of the healing quailities of the awakened Kundalini. Some of the Israelites even began to worship this symbol, and the practice of worshipping the brazen serpent on the pole as a god was either passed on, or was revived later. Bronze and stone serpent artifacts have been found in excavations in Canaan, Gezer and other parts of Israel!

The Old Testament symbol becomes significant in christianity when Christ suggests Kundalini awakening, not just for the tribe of Israel but as the true destiny of all Christians: "And as Moses lifted up the serpent in the wilderness, even as the son of man be lifted up: That whosoever believeth in him should not perish but have eternal life"

He says unequivocally in the Gnostic Gospel of Thomas and elsewhere, that 'The Holy Spirit is My Mother'. 'The Kingdom of God is within you'.

1.1.6. Tao Te Ching

In the Tao Te Ching the primordial power is described as that of a mother. Lao Tze described Kundalini as the "spirit of the valley" (in which flows the Nadi of

Sushumna). The spirit of the valley never dies. The spiritual instrument within us can be described as a microcosm (miniature form of creation) which links us with the Divine. The ancient esoteric text "Scripture of the Golden Flower" also spoke of the effects of the awakened kundalini enerhy.

1.1.7. Buddhist

The Lord Buddha spoke of the "middle path" to achieve nirvana. He was actually describing the central channel (sushumna) through which the Kundalinii ascends. Later Buddhist masters considered that the existence of the path of liberation within a human being was the greatest secret. They transmitted it to only a few deserving disciples.

2

THE KUNDALINI— A RIGHT PERSPECTIVE

2.1. BIRD'S-EYE VIEW

Since the civilization developed, Kundalini or the awakening of the dormant energy has been a mystique subject for the saints, yogis and the scholars. But, it is, in fact, not a child's play and requires self-discipline and the controlling of all senses as well as the proper guidance of a competent spiritual teacher. The so called yogis who claim themselves the proficient in this subject, dare awakening the dormant energy, face serious consequences. So one should be very careful while thinking of awakening the Kundalini. The most important thing in deciding to get to this path, one should rein the anger, sexual instincts, jealousy and arrogance etc. Moreover, one must have strong will power to overcome all these vices which may, otherwise, hamper the development of the proper energy field in a *Sadhak*. There are so many ways recommended in attaining Kundalini yoga, but no single way is perfect in itself as each of the method has its difficulties and limitations. Kundalini yoga combines most of them in a balanced and scientific way so that the awakening of the dormant energy may take place swiftly and without problems, and in a single lifetime. There is a balanced development of personality—physical, mental, emotional and spiritual in this process. So many diseases are also cured as a natural by-product of the Kundalini. Whatever spiritual path one may follow, one experiences a 'great explosion' due to the awakening of the Kundalini, sooner or later, which shifts one into another dimension of the world. It is a journey from the known to the unknown; ordinary consciousness becomes transcendental through the transformation of perceptions, feelings and experiences since the dormant energy rises up and passes through various chakras.

As this dormant energy is in the process of rising, appetite for food and sleep gradually decreases. The mind becomes calm and experiences the tranquility, views various colourful lights and also hears various sounds. The five negatives—lust, anger, greed, attachment and ego get precipitated in degrees but soon subsides completely. Some practitioners obtain psychic powers like clair voyance, clair audience, telepathy, healing power, precognition, levitation etc., but these powers may be short-lived and one should not pay any attention to them. Visions, poetic emotions, artistic perceptions etc., can also be observed in variations and one often makes use of them in self-expression. During its initial process, some people experience terrible headaches, but this is generally experienced to those who have not cleared their blockages of negative energy from their chakras or energy chakras. All these manifestations can be seen because the brain, which hitherto active to only 4 to 6 per cent now experiences the awakening of its silent areas. However, the changes or the disturbances settle down gradually but the awareness becomes very vast, transcending the normal categories and the scope knowledge becames greater. One may develop a special kind of faculty of his brain. A yogi who has obtained or awakened this dormant energy, overcomes the sleep and diverts his all energy in constructive way. At this stage the man who has experienced the Kundalini, passes through a transition period, finds a number of changes emotionally, mentally and physically, but subsides his all explosive energy with calmness and smoothness. This person remains cheerful because his happiness does not depend on external factors anymore. The sources of happiness or bliss which has so far been latent, has now involved in full bloom. One acquires perfect health as a natural by-product and looks much younger than one's real age. He looks graceful in his appearance. Now, he does not feel any fear of death as he has already experienced astral journeys during its process.

2.2 RENOWNED YOGIS

It has already been discussed that there are so many ways to reach the ultimate stage to attain the Kundalini. There have been a number of yogis whom we know and the unknown yogis who do not reveal themselves, experienced the dormant energy awakened. The awakening of the dormant energy or the Kundalini brings various kind of miracles to the common man. It may seen very surprising to some people the music is one of the ways that lead to awakening of this energy. When the music vibrations are taken from navel chakra to the throat chakra repeatedly, the awakening of the Kundalini is experienced. The famous renowned practitioners of music— Swami Haridasa and Tansen are the best examples of this field. The miracles realized by their music are well known.

Chaitanya Mahaprabhu spontaneously attained the level of Kundalini sublimation just by chanting the name of Shri Krishna. He would remain in the same level all time, enjoying the nectar of divine energy. In the same way Swami Ram Krishana Param Hans, lived in Calcutta 130 years ago, experienced the same sublimation. He was a devotee of Maha Kali and attained the grace of the goddess by awakening his Kundalini Swami Ram Krishna Param Hans transferred his power in Swami Vivekananda by a special process, Shaktipat.

Shukdevji awakened his Kundalini at the age of 16. He would remain engrossed in the divine sublimation all the time. Once he was going naked through a forest, when he was passing by a river bank, some women were taking bath. They paid him respect without concerning about his nudity. His old father, Maharshi Ved Vyasji was also trailing behind him. Seeing Vyas Muni, the ladies in scanty clothes started covering them. Muni Vyas was surprised to have seen the changed behaviour of the ladies. The Muni asked the reason. Then the ladies very humbly replied that Mahatma Shukhdev was totally oblivion of the external world: due to his own divine sublimation, but contrarily, the Muni has the full knowledge of the world and the surroundings.

2.3. KEY TO AWAKEN KUNDALINI

There are certain pre-conditions to hold the key to success in awakening Kundalini. These conditions are to be proficient enough doing Moolbandh, Udyein Bandh and Jalandhar Bandh in order to control all the senses of the body. Of them Moolbandh is the most important. The yogic practice is a mystique and miraculous to prepare the body to bear the explosion of the dormant energy being awakened. The Moolbandh itself a comprehensive yogic practice, leads to all round development of the yogis. Most of the people neglecting this step, want to awaken the Kundalini that explodes in a dangerous way as the Moolbandh prepares the body to awaken the Kundalini and most importantly it protects the body from any harms and problems.

For doing Moolbandh, which has already been discussed in the preceding chapters, "Hui yins" point is very significant. This lies between the anus and the genitals. For doing Moolbandh, you must do the maximum practice of contracting the muscles upwards everyday in order to receive the energy in your body. Also you may practise contracting these muscles while you go about in the routine activities. As you continue, it will become easier and easier and you will be able to contract them for longer periods of time. Your muscular coordination will develop so that you will be able to isolate the different muscle groups into back, middle, and front. It is the middle area that is important to hold for generating energy and expanding the energy field of the body. This exercise is similar to the hagel birth exercise for women. Thus Moolbandh is the key to success in awakening the Kundalini. This may successful learnt from some yoga masters or some spiritual teachers who are well versed in this yogic art.

2.4. SYMPTOMS OF AWAKENING

There are number of people who presently boastfully claim that they have awakened their Kundalini. There are some common symptoms, through which one can infer that the Kundalini has awakened in a person, being given below. However, not all the symptoms will appear in every one rather, different symptoms may appear in different persons according to their faculties being developed.

- When the Kundalini awakened the man, under the influence of, eternal bliss, the man becomes very calm, humble, and stays in that position.
- When the Root chakra or Mooladhar awakens, the whole body vibrates, the man should take the deep breathing and he should simply witness the changes taking place.

— The 'ki' or life force begins rising up through the spine and it gives a blissful feeling.

— It has also been found that the body starts trembling, hair standing on end, involuntary laughing or weeping, seeing brightening, visions, uttering deformed sounds or even ejaculations of semen.

— One indulges in involuntary physical actions of the body such spinning, jumping like a frog or lying on the ground like a dead person.

— On awakening of the dormant energy, one sometimes specially in the night feels flying at a very height speed in the air.

— Vibrations of life energy (Prana) at energy centres (chakras), makes one feel that the energy is flowing in the direction of one's thoughts and one may feel electrical jerks in the nerves.

— One feels that the life force is active in the body all the time and a feeling of ecstasy and bliss permeats throughout, even in sleep.

— The arousal of Kundalini intoxicates the person with the divine love, and the person likes to remain in solitude without talking to anybody.

— On Kundalini awakening, one develops various faculties of the brain, can become clairvoyant, inhale divine smells and tastes, hear divine sounds experience divine torch and also instructions from within while doing meditation.

— One experiences insomnia on awakening of Kundalini, can remain without sleeping for months.

— The yogi who has awakened his Kundalini can forecast develops the faculty to know about past, future and can see beyond space.

- One becomes very good orator and develops a miraculous confidence in doing anything.
- Some people feel that a spirit has possessed or haunted as they involuntarily perform certain yoga postures without any pains or fatigue and also possess buoyant energy.
- The gaze fixes on the third eye (Ajna Chakra) while one perform Khechari Mudra. (cessation of breathing and diving into the ocean of bliss is experienced as a result of doing deep meditation).
- During the time of awakening of Kundalini, one may feel whirling in his body and feels an electrical energy speedily going upwards through the spine and the whole energy reaches at Ajna Chakra where he sees various figures. Seeing these figures, sometimes the sadhak is distracted and leaves the practice incomplete.
- The most important symptom of a person who claims that he has experienced the Kundalini, is that he can survive for months without sleeping and breathing. He completely controls the breathing exercises and can remain for months with inhaling and exhaling practices. He must be proficient in controlling the vibrations of Pranas.

2.5 DIFFERENT WAYS OF AWAKENING KUNDALINI

There are different ways of awakening Kundalini the — Bhakti Yoga, Jnana Yoga, Hatha Yoga, Tapasya, Pranayama, Kriya Yoga, Tantra and Shaktipat. These methods have been adopted by yogis to attain the Kundalini Yoga since ancient period. If different methods are practised simultaneously by a yogi it can facilitate the awakening of the Kundalini easily and swiftly. Still there are such type of yogis who receive this power awakened by birth. Sometimes, a person is born with a partial power, called saint. The reason may have been, is that his process was left incomplete in his previous lifetime. Sometime, we may come across to a person who is born with full awakening. He is known as incarnation or Avatar. Such persons are calm detached, compassion, carefree and having divine powers.

2.5.1. Bhakti Yoga

It is the path of devotions, meant for persons who surrender to the God. Mirabai is the best example. She had forgotten and given up everything for the sake of the Lord Krishna. Even the poison could not harm her. Such persons visualize, think and feel that the Lord is present before them and they pour out their manifest love to God in various ways. Ultimately, a continuous flow of awareness takes place between the devotee and the God. This facilitates the awakening of Kundalini and the higher consciousness and a deep state of samadhi is experienced.

2.5.2. Jnana Yoga

This method is meant for the yogis whose mind is more developed rather than the heart. They take everything logically and analytically. Such persons withdraw their mind and emotions from perceiving life and oneself in a deluded way, so that one may behold and live in attunement with the "spirit. They are struck at one question—"who am I." Whenever a thought or feeling arises, which is not the goal, the practitioner says, "neti, neti"— "not this, not this," and discards the sense distraction, concepts, image, sound, until the mind is clear and soul is revealed. This also eventually leads to the path of Kundalini.

2.5.3. Hath-Yoga

There have been a large number of yogis who have been very stubborn without using heart and mind. The development of this path was taken place by Guru Gorakh Nath and Matseyndra Nath in medieval period. In this process, through yogic exercises one can develop a healthy body and pursue the goal of spiritual realization. Through clear mind, healthy body one can meditate and harmonize the body currents of feeling, thinking, willing and acting. In this process various Asanas are recommended in order to awaken the Kundalini through regular practice.

2.5.4. Mantra Yoga

The hymns or the mantras have the miraculous power to awaken the specific chakra, or the energy centre, if they are chanted correctly with right syllables, or words or phrases, like. Om Namah Shivay, Om Mani Padme Hum (A budhist hymn) Soham, and other various mantras. It requires time, patience and guidance of a competent spiritual teacher. Just as a stone thrown into a lake creates circular ripples even so a mantra repeated a million time creates vibrations in the ocean of mind. Eventually it develops the vision of a "higher force" and enables one to live in the midst of sensualities of life with an indifference towards them. There are a large number of mantras or hymns from Sanskrit that can attune one to the Lord and connect one to the realms of "higher consciousness". Each mantra is usually a result of revelations by some mystique vibrations. Kundalini awakens methodically and systematically. Each mantra has different effect on different chakras.

Every word has its own significance. When you express some words expounding your affects or love for anybody that gives a soothing affect on the person, but on the other hand when you abuse somebody, he will instantly react angrily. So every word becomes mantra expressing some emotion, intentions or purpose.

"Nam" is holy word given by the Hindu sages to their devotees to chant silently all day—because the word "N" by its resonant sonic vibrations strengthens the left brain, the eyes and the pituitary gland. The word "M" being the seed word for Crown Chakra, strengthens the upper right brain and the pineal gland and comes to the rescue of left brain whenever, necessary, to calm and soothe the mind by releasing melatonin hormonine. Thus, the word NAM stimulates the total brain. Besides it, 'NAM' helps to boost our immune system.

Apart from it the vedic mantras give out a powerful effect according to the vedic prescriptions. In the same way each chakra has its individual seed Mantra which can generate the energy and activate the chakra when they are chanted repeatedly.

Crown Chakra	
Ajna Chakra	Om.
Throat Chakra	Hum.
Heart Chakra	Yam.
Solar plexus	Rum.
Hara	Wam.
Root Chakra	Lam

2.5.5. Rajyog

This is called kingly path which generally follows the practice of Hath Yoga and vedic methods for a long time. Following this path, the practitioner can do meditation regularly concentrating his consciousness on Ajna chakra or third eye. 'After a long practice, he begins to visualize the various colour and sometime the undefined figures. Eventually the light in the forehead "blazes brighter than the sun". He should be careful not to overstrains the mind with excessive concentration, which can create a split or may lead to severe headache. During the practice the practitioner concentrate on various chakra.

2.5.6. Kriya Yog

The next best alternative to awaken the kundalini is kriya yog which is safer and more practical method. This method is suitable for the householders since Raj Yog is meant for the purific and disciplined people. This is a fact that Kundalini gradually rises. It never goes up violently. When this dormant energy is in the process of awakening, certain changes are manifested like eating too much or very little eating. While doing the practice, the practitioner may experience the insomnia and sometimes he sleeps a lot. It involves a set of yogic asanas that lead to spiritual experience in a controlled way.

2.5.7. Shaktipat

The Shaktipat is a process that awakens the Kundalini instantly without much efforts. The competent spiritual teacher transfers his spiritual power in the eligible person. The Shaktipat is done by transferring his vibrations into the practitioner by touch, by gazing, or by some other mystique method, depending on the system mastered by the spiritual teacher. Swami Ram Krishna Paramhans passed his power and awakened the Kundalini of Swami Vivekananda just by touching him with his toe. Reiki is one the most common and successful system tied to facilitate the path of Kundalini awakening though it is a mild and slower method but is very safer and successful if it is practised regularly and religiously. Reiki takes only an attunement while other disciplines may take years of study and practice. Just as kundalini Shakti, also known as mother Goddess, brings higher consciousness into form even so, Ki (Energy) in Reiki is the goddess of consciousness. Which sets a connection between the physical and spiritual through energy. Kundalini is the female principle of existence even so ki (energy) in Reiki on earth is also the female principle representing yin (female energy). Ki descends from the Higher Consciousness through meditation. Then the energy travels from the hand of the healer into the body of the patient being healed.

However, Kundalini is comparable to fast air travel carrying good results with some risks, while Reiki is safe and slow like land travel and with limited results. Therefore, an alternative and milder method to Kundalini awakening is Reiki. Its attunement opens the three energy channels and chakras and opens the energy on both Sushmna (etheric) and Hara (Swadhisthan chakra) levels. Thus, Reiki is a Kundalini discipline in a controlled way.

Thus, the Reiki, which is better known as "Hasta sparsh chikitsa" in Atharveda and other vedic texts, is a Kundalini discipline in a controlled way. This is being practised at three levels. In Reiki—I, alongwith the basic principles, the repeated attunements increase the capacity of the chakra to hold the ki, which is further used to heal the patient and also it evolves the basic energy level. The Reiki-II takes the person further and is much more powerful than the former. In Reiki-III, the person leaps further to experience the Kundalini awakening gradually. But, as a matter of fact, it requires very intense practice of meditation.

I like to conclude with this note the Kundalini awakening has been a mystique science for which yogis, since ancient period, have been preparing themselves to evolve, but, one must not take up the practice without consulting a competent teacher. Reiki, in the modern time, is a milder but, very simple way to evolve our energy level or field to prepare further to awaken the dormant energy. This is also a truth, once this energy is awakened, the yogi experiences the miracles that cannot be thought about by a common person.

3

IMPORTANCE OF KUNDALINI YOGA

The word 'Yoga' comes from a Sanskrit root *'Yuj'* which means to join. In its spiritual sense it is that process by which the identity of the Jivatma and Paramatma is realised by the Yogins. The human soul is brought into conscious communion with God. Yoga is restraining the mental modifications. Yoga is that inhibition of the functions of the mind which leads to abidance of the spirit in his real nature. The inhibition of these functions of the mind is by Abhyasa and Vairagya" (Yoga Sutras).

Yoga is the Science that teaches the method of joining the human spirit with God. Yoga is the Divine Science which disentangles the Jiva from the phenomenal world of sense-objects and links him with the *Ananta Ananda* (Infinite Bliss), *Parama Shanti* (Supreme Peace), joy of an Akhanda character and Power that are inherent attributes of the Absolute. Yoga gives Mukti through Asamprajnata Samadhi by destroying all the Sankalpas of all antecedent mental functions. No Samadhi is possible without awakening the Kundalini. When the Yogi attains the highest stage, all his Karmas are burnt and he gets liberation from Samsara-Chakra.

Kundalini Yoga is a meditative discipline —or a system of meditative techniques and movements—within the yogic tradition that focuses on psycho-spiritual growth and the body's potential for maturation. The practice of Kundalini Yoga consists of a number bodily postures, expressive movements and utterances, characterological cultivations, breathing patterns, and degrees of concentration. The movements and the body-work should not—according to some scholars of religion—be considered mere stretching exercises.

The concept of life-energy—pranotthana—is central to the practice and understanding of Kundalini Yoga. It also gives special consideration to the role of the spine and the endocrine system in the understanding of yogic awakening. Recently, there has been a growing interest within the medical community to study the physiological effects of meditation, and some of these studies have applied the discipline of Kundalini Yoga to their clinical settings.

3.1. RISING KUNDALINI

Kundalini is supposed to be raised through meditative exercises and activated within the concept of a subtle body, a body of energy and finer substance. As the Kundalini raises from the root-chakra up through the spinal channel, called sushumna, it is believed to activate each chakra it goes through. Each chakra is said to contain special characteristics, and although the opening of higher chakras are believed to mark advanced spiritual unfoldment, it is important not to measure spiritual growth solely by the opening of higher potentials.

According to this view chakras might be under- or overdeveloped, and lower chakras are thought to be just as important as higher. In raising Kundalini, spiritual powers (siddhis) are also believed to arise, but many spiritual traditions see these phenomena as obstacles on the path, and encourages their students not to get hung up with them.

Any form of intense contemplative or spiritual practice without the support of a cultural context, or without the support of thorough psychological preparation, is usually considered to be unfortunate, and in some cases even dangerous. Initiation of kundalini activity is usually considered to take place by a form of 'laying on of hands', or shaktipat, where physical contact to the body or the forehead of the subject by the guru or initiator is supposed to cause an experience of Kundalini that later may persist or grow with continuing practice, or fade away if practice is neglected.

Kundalini as a spiritual experience is thought to have parallels in many of the mystical and gnostic traditions of the world's great religions. Many factors point to the universality of the phenomenon. The early Christians might have referred to the concept as 'pneuma', and there are some recent parallells in contemporary Christian charismatic 'Holy Ghost' phenomena. Religious studies also note parallels in Quakerism, Shakerism, Judaic davening (torso-rocking prayer), the swaying zikr and whirling dervish of Islam, the quiverings of the Eastern Orthodox hesychast, the flowing movements of tai chi, the ecstatic shamanic dance, the ntum trance dance of the Bushman, Tibetan Buddhist tummo heat as practised by Milarepa, and the Indically-derived Andalusian flamenco.

3.2. KUNDALINI SYNDROME

A complex pattern of motor, sensory, affective and cognitive/hermeneutic symptoms called The Kundalini Syndrome. This psycho-somatic arousal and excitation is believed to occur in connection with prolonged and intensive spiritual or contemplative practice (such as meditation or yoga) or as a result of intense life experiences or a close encounter with death (such as a near-death experience). The Kundalini-syndrome is a process that might unfold over several months, or even years. If the accompagnying symptoms unfold in an intense manner—that de-stabilizes the person—the process is usually interpreted as a Spiritual Emergency.

Motor symptoms are thought to include tremors, shaking, spontaneous or involuntary body-movements and changes in respiratory function. Sensory symptoms are thought to include changes in body-temperature (feelings of heat or cold), a feeling of energy running along the spine or progressing upwards in the body, a feeling of electricity in the body, headache and pressure inside of the head, tingling, vibrations and gastro-intestinal problems.

Cognitive and affective symptoms are thought to include psychological upheaval, stress, depre-ssion,depersonalisation or derealisation, intense mood-swings, altered states of consciousness (trance-like experiences), hallucinations (inner visions or acoustical phenomena), but also moments of bliss and deep peace. A roaring noise or other loud auditory hallucination have also been reported, perhaps related to the phenomenon of 'Exploding head syndrome'. Within the mentioned academic traditions this symptomatology is often referred to as the Physio-Kundalini syndrome or Kundalini-experience/awakening.

3.3. CHAKRAS IN YOGA

The seven Chakras, in Yoga, are basically power points or vortices, such as the Kundalini, through which various energies are received, distributed, and transformed. There is no scientific evidence to support the existence of literal Chakras. In reality, they are symbolic states of consciousness that most followers of Hindu beliefs have accepted as real.

There are seven etheric Chakras which many believe to be located in the following parts of the body: the root (base of the spine), the sacral, the solar plexus, the heart, the throat, the brow, and the crown. Many have thought Chakras are literally in the body when there is no scientific evidence to support their existence or their aid in the operation of the various bodily systems. When one understands their meaning, one can see that they are symbolic.

1. The root is located at the base of the spine, which is the seat of the Kundalini. This Chakra is concerned with animal instincts such as self-preservation, taste and smell.
2. The second Chakra lies nears the genital area and governs sexuality and reproduction. It is believed to govern digestion.
3. The solar plexus Chakra is just above the navel. It is often associated with emotions. It is believed to affect the liver, pancreas, and stomach.
4. The heart Chakra is located in the center of the chest. It is the first Chakra to be linked with higher consciousness and unconditional love. It is also associated with the pituitary gland, pineal gland.
5. The throat Chakra is associated with creativity and causes the search for truth.
6. The Anja Chakra is located between the eyebrows and is called the "third eye" for it influences psychic senses, such as intuition.
7. The crown Chakra whirls just above the head. It reveals the individual level of consciousness. When this Chakra is activated, it brings supreme illumination.

The seven Chakras gave the audience an idea of what they are and what they symbolically represent. The audience was also able to see that the seven Chakras were activated in an ascension manner resulting in the individual's consciousness being raised. One can also see that these Chakras are symbolical and not literally in the body.

In Kundalini Yoga the creating and sustaining Sakti of the whole body is actually and truly united with Lord Siva. The Yogi goads Her to introduce him to Her Lord. The rousing of Kundalini Sakti and Her Union with Lord Siva effects the state of *Samadhi* (Ecstatic union) and spiritual *Anubhava* (experience). It is She who gives Knowledge or Jnana, for She is Herself That. Kundalini Herself, when awakened by the Yogins, achieves for them the Jnana (illumination).

Kundalini can be awakened by various means and these different methods are called by different names, viz., Raja Yoga, Hatha Yoga, etc. The practitioner of this Kundalini Yoga claims, that it is higher than any other process and that Samadhi attained thereby is more perfect. The reason that they allege, is this:—In Dhyana Yoga, ecstasy takes place through detachment from the world and mental concentration leading the variety of mental operation (*Vritti*) of the uprising of pure consciousness unhindered by the limitations of the mind. The degree to which this unveiling of consciousness is effected, depends upon the meditative power, Dhyana Sakti, of the Sadhaka and the extent of detachment from the world.

On the other hand, Kundalini is all Sakti and is therefore Jnana Sakti Herself—bestows Jnana and Mukti, when awakened by the Yogins. Secondly, in Kundalini Yoga there is not merely a Samadhi through meditation, but the central power of the Jiva, carries with it the forms of both body and mind. The union in that sense is claimed to be more complete than that enacted through methods only. Though in both cases the body-consciousness is lost, in Kundalini Yoga not only the mind but the body also, in so far as it is represented by its central power, is actually united with Lord Siva at the Sahasrara Chakra. This union (Samadhi) produces *Bhukti* (enjoyment) which a Dhyana Yogi does not possess.

A Kundalini Yogi has both *Bhukti* (enjoyment) and *Mukti* (liberation) in the fullest and literal sense. Hence this Yoga is claimed to be the foremost of all Yogas. When the sleeping Kundalini is awakened by Yogic Kriyas, it forces a passage upwards through the different Chakras (Shat-Chakra *Bheda*). It excites or stimulates them into intense activity. During its ascent, layer after layer of the mind becomes fully opened. All *Kleshas* (afflictions) and the three kinds of Taapa will vanish. The Yogi experiences various visions, powers, bliss and knowledge. When it reaches Sahasrara Chakra in the brain, the Yogi gets the maximum knowledge, Bliss, power and Siddhis. He reaches the highest rung in the Yogic ladder. He gets perfectly detached from body and mind. He becomes free in all respects. He is a full-blown Yogi (*Purna Yogi*).

3.3.1. Sadhakas

When the whole vitality is sapped from the body one cannot do any rigid Sadhana. Youth is the best period for Yoga Abhyasa. This is the first and the foremost qualification of a Sadhaka; there must be vigour and vitality. One who has a calm mind, who has faith in the words of his Guru and Sastras, who is moderate in eating and sleeping and who has the intense longing for deliverance from the Samsara-Chakra is a qualified person for the practice of Yoga.

Those who are addicted to sensual pleasures or those who are arrogant and proud, dishonest, untruthful, diplomatic, cunning and treacherous and who disrespect the Guru, Sadhus and elders and take pleasure in vain controversies and worldly actions, can never attain success in Yogic practices. Kama, Krodha, Lobha, Moha, Mada, and all other impurities should be completely annihilated. One cannot become pure and perfect when one has so many impure qualities.

Sadhakas should develop the following virtuous qualities:

1. Straightforwardness, service to Guru, the sick and old persons, Ahimsa, Brahmacharya, spontaneous generosity, Titiksha, Sama Drishti, Samata, spirit of service, selflessness, tolerance, Mitahara, humility, honesty and other virtues to an enormous degree. Aspirants will not at all be benefited in any way in the absence of these virtues even if they exert much to awaken the Kundalini through Yogic exercises.
2. Aspirants should freely open their hearts to their Guru. They must be frank and candid. They should give up the self-assertive, Rajasic vehemence, vanity and arrogance, and carry out their master's instructions with Sraddha and Prem. Constant self-justification is a dangerous habit for a Sadhaka.
3. Energy is wasted in too much talking, unnecessary worry and vain fear. Gossiping and tall-talk should be given up entirely. A real Sadhaka is a man of few words, to the point and that too on spiritual matters only. Sadhakas should always remain alone. Mouna is a great *desideratum.* Mixing with householders is highly dangerous for a Sadhaka. The company of a householder is far more injurious than the company of a woman. Mind has the power to imitate.

3.3.2. Diet of a Yogi

A Sadhaka should observe perfect discipline. He must be civil, polite, courteous, gentle, noble and gracious in his behaviour. He must have perseverance, adamantine will, asinine patience and *leech-like tenacity* in Sadhana. He must be perfectly self-controlled, pure and devoted to the Guru.

Food plays a prominent place in Yoga-Sadhana. An aspirant should be very careful in the selection of articles of Sattvic nature especially in the beginning of his Sadhana period. Later on when Siddhi is attained, drastic dietetic restrictions can be removed. Purity of food leads to purity of mind. Sattvic food helps meditation. The discipline of food is very very necessary for Yogic Sadhana. If the tongue is controlled, all the other Indriyas are controlled.

By the purity of food follows the purification of the inner nature, by the purification of the nature, memory becomes firm and on strengthening the memory, follows the loosening of all ties and the wise get Moksha thereby."

Charu: Boil half a seer of milk along with some boiled rice, ghee and sugar. This is an excellent food for Yogins. This is for the day-time. For the night, half a seer of milk will do.

Milk should not be too much boiled. It should be removed from the fire as soon as the boiling point is reached. Too much boiling destroys the nutritious principles and vitamins and renders it quite useless. This is an ideal food for Sadhakas. Milk is a perfect food by itself.

A fruit diet exercises a benign influence on the constitution. This is a natural form of diet. Fruits are very great energy-producers. Fruits and milk diet help concentration and easy mental focussing. Barley, wheat, milk and ghee promote longevity and increase power and strength. Fruit-juice and the water wherein sugar-candy is dissolved, are very good beverages. Butter mixed with sugar-candy, and almonds soaked in water can be taken. These will cool the system.

Rajasic food distracts the mind. It excites passion. Give up salt. It excites passion and emotion. Giving up of salt helps in controlling the tongue and thereby the mind and in developing will-power also. Snake-bite and scorpion-stings will have no influence on a man who has given up salt. Onions and garlic are worse than meat.

Live a natural life. Take simple food that is agreeable. You should have your own menu to suit your constitution. You are yourself the best judge to select a Sattvic diet. The proficient in Yoga should abandon articles of food detrimental to the practice of Yoga. During intense Sadhana, milk (and ghee also) is ordained.

Milk is the best food for Yogins. But even a small quantity of milk is harmful for some and may not agree with all constitutions. If one form of diet is not suitable or if you feel constipated, change the diet and try some other Sattvic articles. This is Yukti. In the matter of food and drinks you should be a master. You should not have the least craving or sense-hankering for any particular food. You must not become a slave to any particular object.

3.3.3. Mitahara

Heavy food leads to Tamasic state and induces sleep only. There is a general misapprehension that a large quantity of food is necessary for health and strength. Much depends upon the power of assimilation and absorption. Generally, in the vast majority of cases, most of the food passes away undigested along with faeces. Take half stomachful of wholesome food. Fill a quarter with pure water. Leave the rest free. This is Mitahara. Mitahara plays a vital part in keeping up perfect health.

Almost all diseases are due to irregularity of meals, overeating and unwholesome food. Eating all things at all times like a monkey is highly dangerous. Such a man can become a Rogi (sick man) easily; but he can never become a Yogi. Hear the emphatic declaration of Lord Krishna: "Success in Yoga is not for him who eats too much or too little; nor for him who sleeps too much or too little. Again in the Sloka 18 of the same chapter, He says: "To him who is temperate in eating and in sleep and wakefulness, Yoga becomes a destroyer of misery."

A glutton cannot at the very outset have diet regulations and observe Mitahara. He must gradually practise this. First let him take less quantity twice as usual. Then instead of the usual heavy night meals, let him take fruits and milk alone for some days. In due course of time he can completely avoid the night meals and try to take fruits and milk in the daytime. Those who do intense Sadhana must take milk alone. It is a perfect food by itself. If necessary they can take some easily digestible fruits.

Do not fast much. It will produce weakness in you. Occasional fasting once a month or when passion troubles you much, will suffice. During fasting you should not even think of the various articles of food. Constant thinking of the food when you fast cannot bring you the desired result. During fasting, avoid company. Live alone. Utilise your time in Yogic Sadhana. After a fast do not take any heavy food. Milk or some fruit-juice is beneficial.

Do not make much fuss about your diet. You need not advertise to everyone if you are able to pull on with a particular form of diet. The observance of such Niyamas is for your advancement in the spiritual path and you will not be spiritually benefited by giving publicity to your Sadhana. There are many nowadays who make it a profession to earn money and their livelihood by performing some Asana, Pranayama or by having some diet regulation such as eating only raw articles or leaves or roots. They cannot have any spiritual growth. The goal of life is Self-realisation. Sadhakas should keep the goal always in view and do intense Sadhana with the prescribed methods.

3.3.3.1. Place for sadhana

Sadhana should be done in a secluded place. There should be no interruption by anyone. When you live in a house, a well-ventilated room should be reserved for Sadhana purposes. Do not allow anybody to enter the room. Keep it under lock and key. Do not allow even your wife, children or intimate friends to enter the room. It should be kept pure and holy. It should be free from mosquitoes, flies and lice and absolutely free from dampness. Do not keep too many things in the room. They will distract you every now and then. No surrounding noise also should disturb you. The room should not be too big as the eyes will begin to wander.

Places of cool or temperate climate are required for Yoga Abhyasa as you will get easily exhausted in hot place. You must select such a place where you can comfortably stay all through the year in winter, summer and rainy season. You must stick to one place throughout Sadhana period. Select a beautiful and pleasant spot where there is no disturbance, on the banks of a river, lake or sea or top of a hill where there is a nice spring and grove of trees and where milk and articles of food are easily procurable.

You should select such a place where there are some other Yogic practitioners. When you see others who are devoted to Yogic practices you will diligently apply yourself to your practices. You can consult them in times of difficulties. Do not wander here and there in search of a place where you will get all conveniences. Do not change your place very often when you find some inconvenience. You must put up with it. Every place has some advantage and disadvantage. Find out a place where you have many advantages and a few disadvantages.

If you build a Kutir in a crowded place, people out of curiosity will disturb you. You will have no spiritual vibrations there. There will be a lot of other disturbances also. Again you will be without any protection if you construct your Kutir in a thick forest. Thieves and wild animals will trouble you. The question of food will arise. You must consider all these points well before you select a place for your Sadhana. If you cannot go in for such places, convert a solitary room into a forest.

Your Asana (seat) for the Yogic practices should not be too high or too low. Spread a seat of *Kusha* grass, tiger-skin or deer-skin and then sit. Burn incense daily in the room. In the initial period of your Sadhana you must be very particular about all these. When you have sufficiently advanced in your practice, then you need not lay much stress on such rules.

3.3.3.2. Time

It is stated in Gheranda Samhita that Yogic practices should not be commenced in winter, summer and rainy seasons, but only in spring and autumn. This depends upon the temperature of the particular place and the strength of the individual. Generally cool hours are best suited. In hot places you should not practise during the day. Early morning hours are suitable for Yogic practices. You should completely avoid Yoga Abhyasa in summer in those places where the temperature is hot even in winter. Generally Yogic practices should be done only after a bath. A bath is not beneficial immediately after the practices. You should not sit for Yogic practices when your mind is restless or when you are worried much.

3.3.3.3. *The Age*

Young boys under 18 years of age whose bodies are very tender should not have too much practice. They have a very tender body which cannot stand the exertion of Yogic exercises. Further, a youth's mind will be wandering and unsettled and so, in youth one cannot concentrate well, whereas, Yogic exercises require intense and deep concentration. In old age when all vitality is sapped by unnecessary worry, anxieties, troubles and other worldly Vyavaharas, one cannot do any spiritual practice. Yoga requires full vitality, energy, power and strength. Therefore the best period for Yoga Abhyasa is from 20 to 40 years of age. Those who are strong and healthy can take to Yogic practices even after 50.

4

IMPORTANCE OF PRANAYAMA

Prana is the sum total of all energy that is manifested in the universe. It is the vital force, Sukshma. Breath is the external manifestation of Prana. By exercising control over this gross breath, you can control the subtle Prana inside. Control of Prana means control of mind. Mind cannot operate without the help of Prana. It is the Sukshma Prana that is intimately connected with the mind. Prana is the sum total of all latent forces which are hidden in men and which lie everywhere around us. Heat, light, electricity, magnetism are all the manifestations of Prana. Prana is related to mind; through mind to the will; through will to the individual soul, and through this to the Supreme Being.

The seat of Prana is the heart. Prana is one; but it has many functions to do. Hence it assumes five names according to the different functions it performs, viz., Prana, Apana, Samana, Udana and Vyana. According to the different functions they perform, they occupy certain places in the body. The table given in the following pages will give you a clear idea.

Breath directed by thought under the control of the will is a vitalising, regenerated force which can be utilised consciously for self-development, for healing many incurable diseases and for many other useful purposes. Hatha Yogins consider that Prana Tattva is superior to Manas Tattva (mind), as Prana is present even when mind is absent during deep sleep. Hence Prana plays a more vital part than mind.

If you know how to control the little waves of Prana working through mind, then the secret of subjugating the universal Prana will be known to you. The Yogin who becomes an expert in the knowledge of this secret, will have no fear from any power, because he has mastery over all manifestations of power in the Universe.

What is commonly known as Power of Personality is nothing more than the natural capacity of a person to wield his Prana. Some people are more powerful in life, more influential and fascinating than others. It is all through this Prana, which the Yogin uses consciously by the command of his will.

Having acquired a thorough knowledge of the seat of Nadis and of the Vayus with their functions, one should begin with the purification of Nadis. A person possessed of Yama and Niyama, avoiding all company, having finished his course of study, delighting in Truth and virtues, having conquered his anger, being engaged in the service of his spiritual instructor and well instructed in all the religious practices, should go to a secluded place for Yoga Abhyasa.

Nadi Suddhi (purification of Nadis) is an important matter in the early stage of Yoga. If there are impurities in the Nadis, the ascent of Kundalini in the Sushumna is seriously retarded. Purity in the Nadis facilitates the ascent of Kundalini. Pranayama brings about quick purification of the Nadis. Nadi Suddhi is the basis of Yoga. It is the foundation of Yoga. It is the first part of Yoga.

Just as you can stop all the other wheels of the factory if you can stop the important fly-wheel of the engine, so also if you can stop the functions of all other organs of the body, you can get control of the subtle, psychic Prana by restraining the breath. That is the reason why Pranayama is prescribed for controlling Prana.

Prana is the over-coat of the mind. If you can control Prana, you can control mind and Veerya also, because Prana, Veerya and mind are under one Sambandha. If you can control mind, breath stops by itself. Prana comes under control.

Just as you have a nervous system in the gross physical body, so also there is a nervous system in the astral body. The nervous system of the physical body is the Sthula Prana. The nervous system of the astral body is the Sukshma Prana. There is intimate connection between these two Pranas. There is inter-action between these two Pranas.

By controlling the act of breathing, you can efficiently control all the various functions in the body. You can very easily and quickly control and develop the body, mind and soul. Psychic cure, Telepathy, Television, thought-reading and other Siddhis are the effects of the control of Prana. The process by which the Prana is controlled by regulation of breath is termed 'Pranayama'. It is through Pranayama that you can control your circumstances and character and consciously harmonise the universal individual life with the cosmic life.

To suit the different constitutions, temperament and purpose, in Pranayama there are many varieties of exercises, viz., deep breathing exercise, Sukha Purvaka (easy comfortable) Pranayama during walking, Pranayama during meditation, Rhythmical breathing, Suryabheda, Ujjayi, Sitkari, Sitali, Bhastrika, Bhramari, Murchha, Plavini, Kevala Kumbhaka, etc. Of all the above exercises only the last eight are described in the Hatha Yogic texts.

4.1. NADI SUDDHI

Before commencing the practice of Pranayama however, you should clean the Nadis. Then only will you derive the maximum benefit from Pranayama. The cleansing of the Nadi (Nadi-Suddhi) is either Samanu or Nirmanu—that is, with or without the use of Bija. According to the first form, the Yogi in Padmasana or Siddhasana offers his prayers to the Guru and meditates on him. Meditating on 'Yang' he does Japa through Ida of the Bija 16 times, Kumbhaka with Japa of the Bija 64 times, and then exhalation through the solar Nadi and Japa of Bija 32 times. Fire is raised from Manipura and united with Prithvi. Then follows inhalation by the solar Nadi with the Vahni Bija 'Rang' 16 times, Kumbhaka with Japa of the Bija 64 times, followed by exhalation through the lunar Nadi and Japa of the Bija 32 times. He then meditates on the lunar brilliance, gazing at the tip of the nose, and inhales by Ida with Japa of the Bija 'Thang' 16 times. Kumbhaka is done with the Bija 'Vang' 64 times. He thinks himself as flooded by nectar, and considers that the Nadis have been washed. He exhales by Pingala with Japa of the Bija 'Lang' 32 times and considers himself thereby as strengthened.

Following are the important exercises for comfortable pranayama:

4.1.1. Sukha Purvaka

Sit in Padmasana or Siddhasana. Close the right nostril with your right thumb. Inhale (Puraka) through the left nostril till you count 3 Oms slowly. Imagine that you are drawing the Prana along with the atmospheric air. In course of practice, you will actually feel that you are drawing Prana. Then close the left nostril also with the little and ring fingers of your right hand. Retain the breath till you count 12 Oms. Send the current down to the Muladhara Chakra. Feel that the nerve-current is striking against the Muladhara Chakra and awakening Kundalini. Remove the right thumb and exhale through the right nostril till you count 6 Oms. Again inhale through the right nostril, retain and exhale through the left nostril as stated above. All the above six processes constitute one Pranayama. To start with do 6 Pranayamas in the morning and 6 in the evening. Gradually increase it to 20 Pranayamas for each sitting. The ratio of inhalation, retention and exhalation is 1:4:2. You should gradually increase the period of Kumbhaka.

Be careful in doing the Kumbhaka as long as you can comfortably do. Do not be in a hurry. Be patient. Contract the anus and do Mula Bandha also. Concentrate on the Chakra and meditate on Kundalini. This is the most important portion of this exercise. In this Pranayama, deep concentration plays a vital part in awakening Kundalini. Kundalini will be awakened quickly if the degree of concentration is intense and if practised regularly.

This exercise removes all diseases, purifies the Nadis, steadies the wandering mind, improves digestion and circulation, helps Brahmacharya, and awakens Kundalini. All the impurities of the body are thrown out.

4.1.2. Bhastrika

Rapid succession of forcible expulsions is a characteristic feature of this exercise. 'Bhastrika' means 'bellows' in Sanskrit. Just as a blacksmith blows his bellows rapidly, so also you should inhale and exhale rapidly. Sit in your favourite Asana. Close the mouth. Inhale and exhale quickly 20 times like the bellows. Constantly dilate and contract the chest as you inhale and exhale. When you practise the Pranayama a hissing sound is produced. You should start with forcible expulsions of breath following one another in rapid succession. After 20 such expulsions, make a deep inhalation and retain the breath as long as you can comfortably do and then slowly exhale. This is one round of Bhastrika.

Begin with 10 expulsions for a round and increase it gradually to 20 or 25 for a round. The period of Kumbhaka also should be gradually and cautiously increased. Rest a while after one round is over and again begin the next round. Do 3 rounds in the beginning and after due practice, do 20 rounds in the morning and 20 in the evening.

Advanced students do this Pranayama after partial closing of the glottis. They do not make a powerful noise like the beginners. They can do it even in a standing posture. Bhastrika removes inflammation of the throat, increases the gastric fire, destroys phlegm and all diseases of the nose and lungs, eradicates Asthma, consumption and other diseases which arise from the excess of wind, bile and phlegm. It gives warmth to the body. It is the most effective of all Pranayama exercises. It enables Prana to break through the three Granthis. All the other benefits of Sukha Purvaka Pranayama are obtained in this exercise also.

4.1.3. Suryabheda

Sit on Padmasana or Siddhasana. Close the eyes. Keep the left nostril closed with your right ring and little fingers. Slowly inhale without making any sound as long as you can do it comfortably through the right nostril. Then close the right nostril with your right thumb and retain the breath by firmly pressing the chin against the chest (Jalandhara Bandha). Hold the breath till perspiration oozes from the roots of the hair (hair follicles). This point cannot be reached at the very outset. You will have to increase the period of Kumbhaka gradually. This is the limit of the sphere of practice of Suryabheda Kumbhaka. Release the Jalandhara Bandha. Then exhale very slowly without making any sound through the left nostril with the thumb closing the right nostril. "The practice of Suryabheda Kumbhaka destroys decay and death and awakens Kundalini."

This Pranayama should again and again be performed, as it purifies the brain and destroys the intestinal worms. It removes the four kinds of evils caused by Vayu and cures Vata (rheumatism). It cures rhinitis and various sorts of neuralgia. The worms that are found in the frontal sinuses are also destroyed.

4.1.4. Ujjayi

Sit in your usual Asana. Close the mouth. Inhale slowly through both the nostrils in a smooth, uniform manner. Retain the breath as long as you can do it comfortably and then exhale slowly through the left nostril by closing the right nostril with your right thumb. Expand the chest when you inhale. During inhalation a peculiar sound is produced owing to the partial closing of glottis. The sound produced during inhalation should be of a mild and uniform pitch. It should be continuous also. This Kumbhaka may be practised even when walking or standing. Instead of exhaling through the left nostril, you can exhale slowly through both nostrils.

This removes the heat in the head. The practitioner becomes very beautiful. The gastric fire is increased. It removes phlegm in the throat. Asthma, consumption and all sorts of pulmonary diseases are cured. All diseases that arise from deficient inhalation of oxygen and diseases of the heart are cured. All works are accomplished by Ujjayi Pranayama. The practitioner is never attacked by diseases of phlegm, nerves, enlargement of spleen, dyspepsia, dysentery, consumption, cough or fever. Perform Ujjayi to destroy decay and death.

4.1.5. Plavini

Practice of this Pranayama demands skill on the part of the students. He who practises this Plavini can do Jalastambha and float on water for any length of time, Mr. 'S', a Yogic student, can float on water for twelve hours at a stretch. He who practises this Plavini Kumbhaka can live on air and dispense with food for some days. The student actually drinks air slowly like water and sends it to the stomach. The stomach gets bloated a bit. If you tap the stomach when it is filled with air, you will get a peculiar tympanic (air) sound. Gradual practice is necessary. The help of one who is well versed in this Pranayama, is necessary. The student can fill up the stomach with air by gradual belching. After the practice, the air should be completely taken out. It is done by Uddiyana Bandha and hiccough.

4.1.6. Pranic Healing

Those who practise Pranayama, can impart their Prana for healing morbid diseases. They can also recharge themselves with Prana in no time by practising Kumbhaka. Never think that you will be depleted of your Prana by distributing it to others. The more you will give, the more it will flow to you from the cosmic source (Hiranyagarbha). That is the law of Nature. Do not become a niggard. If there is a rheumatic patient, gently shampoo his legs with your hands. When you do shampooing (massage), do Kumbhaka and imagine that the Prana is flowing from your hands towards your patient.

Connect yourself with Hiranyagarbha or the cosmic Prana and imagine that the cosmic energy is flowing through your hands towards the patient. The patient will at once feel warmth, relief and strength. You can cure headache, intestinal colic or any other disease by massage and by your magnetic touch. When you massage the liver, spleen, stomach or any other portion or organ of the body you can speak to the cells and give them orders. Discharge your functions properly. I command you to do so." They will obey your orders—O'cell, Discharge your functions properly. They too have got subconscious intelligence. Repeat your Mantra when you pass your Prana to others. Try a few cases. You will gain competence. You can cure scorpion-sting also. Gently shampoo the leg and bring the poison down.

You can have extraordinary power of concentration, strong will and a perfectly healthy, strong body by practising Pranayama regularly. You will have to direct the Prana consciously to unhealthy parts of the body. Suppose you have a sluggish liver. Sit on Padmasana. Close your eyes. Do Sukha Purvaka Pranayama. Direct the Prana to the region of the liver. Concentrate your mind there. Fix your attention to that area. Imagine that Prana is interpenetrating all the tissues and the cells of the lobes of the liver and doing its curative, regenerating and constructive work there. Faith, imagination, attention and interest play a very important part in curing diseases by taking Prana to the diseased areas.

During exhalation imagine that the morbid impurities of the liver are thrown out. Repeat this process 12 times in the morning and 12 times in the evening. Sluggishness of liver will vanish in a few days. This is a drugless treatment. This is nature-cure. You can take the Prana to any part of the body during the Pranayama and cure any kind of disease, be it acute or chronic. Try once or twice in healing yourself. Your convictions will grow stronger. Why do you cry like the lady who is crying for ghee when she has butter in her hand, when you have a cheap, potent, easily available remedy or agent 'Prana' at your command at all times! Use it judiciously. When you advance in your concentration and practice, you can cure many diseases by mere touch. In the advanced stages, many diseases are cured by mere will.

4.1.7. Distant Healing

This is known as "absent treatment" also. You can transmit Prana through space to your friend who is living at a distance. He should have a receptive mental attitude. You must feel yourself *en rapport* (in direct relation and in sympathy) with the people whom you heal with this Distant Healing method.

You can fix hours of appointment with them through correspondence. You can write to them: "Get ready at 8 p.m. Have a receptive mental attitude. Lie down in an easy-chair. Close your eyes. I shall transmit my Prana".

Say mentally to the patient, 'I am transmitting a supply of Prana (vital force)'. Do Kumbhaka when you send the Prana. Practise rhythmical breathing also. Have a mental image that the Prana is leaving your mind, passing through space, and is entering the system of the patient. The Prana travels unseen like the wireless (radio) waves and flashes like lightning across space. The Prana that is coloured by the thought of the healer is projected outside. You can re-charge yourself with Prana by practising Kumbhaka. This requires long, steady and regular practice.

Tamas and Rajas constitute the covering or veil. This veil is removed by the practice of Pranayama. After the veil is removed, the real nature of the soul is realised. The Chitta is by itself made up of Sattvic particles, but it is enveloped by Rajas and Tamas, just as the fire is enveloped by smoke. There is no purificatory action greater than Pranayama. Pranayama gives purity, and the light of knowledge shines. The Karma of the Yogi, which covers up the discriminative knowledge, is annihilated by the practice of Pranayama. By the magic panorama of desire, the essence, which is luminous by nature, is covered up and the Jiva or individual soul is directed towards vice. This Karma of the Yogi which covers up the Light and binds him to repeated births, becomes attenuated by the practice of Pranayama every moment and is destroyed eventually.

Dharanasu cha Yogyata Manasah: "The mind becomes fit for concentration"—Yoga Sutra. You will be able to concentrate the mind nicely after this veil of the light has been removed. The mind will be quite steady like the flame in a windless place as the disturbing energy has been removed. The word Pranayama is sometimes used collectively for inhalation, retention and exhalation of breath and sometimes for each of these severally. When the Prana Vayu moves in Akasa Tattva, the breathing will be lessened. At this time it will be easy to stop the breath. The velocity of the mind will be slowly lessened by the Pranayama. It will induce Vairagya also.

4.2. ADVANTAGES OF PRANAYAMA

This body becomes lean, strong and healthy. Too much fat is reduced. There is lustre in the face. Eyes sparkle like diamonds. The practitioner becomes very handsome. Voice becomes sweet and melodious. The inner Anahata sounds are distinctly heard. The student is free from all sorts of diseases. He gets established in Brahmacharya. Semen gets firm and steady. The Jatharagni (gastric fire) is augmented. The student becomes so perfected in Brahmacharya that his mind will not be shaken even if a fairy tries to embrace him. Appetite becomes keen. Nadis are purified. Vikshepa is removed and the mind becomes one-pointed. Rajas and Tamas are destroyed. The mind is prepared for Dharana and Dhyana. The excretions become scanty. Steady practice arouses the inner spiritual force and brings in spiritual light, happiness and peace of mind. It makes him an Oordhvareto-Yogi. All psychic powers are obtained. Advanced students only will get all the benefits.

4.2.1. Instructions

1. Early morning, answer the calls of nature and sit for the Yogic practices. Practise Pranayama in a dry, welt-ventilated room. Pranayama requires deep concentration and attention. Do not keep anyone by your side.
2. Before you sit for Pranayama practice, thoroughly clean the nostrils. When you finish the practice, take a cup of milk or light tiffin after 10 minutes.
3. Strictly avoid too much talking, eating, sleeping, mixing with friends and exertion. Take a little ghee with rice when you take your meals. This will lubricate the bowels and allow Vayu to move downwards freely.
4. Some people twist the muscles of the face when they do Kumbhaka. It should be avoided. It is also a symptom to indicate that they are going beyond their capacity. This must be strictly avoided. Such people cannot have a regulated Rechaka and Puraka.
5. Pranayama can also be performed as soon as you get up from bed and just before Japa and meditation. It will make your body light and you will enjoy the meditation. You must have a routine according to your convenience and time.
6. Do not shake the body unnecessarily. By shaking the body often the mind also is disturbed. Do not

scratch the body every now and then. The Asana should be steady and as firm as a rock when you do Pranayama, Japa and meditation.

7. In all the exercises, repeat Rama, Siva, Gayatri, or any other Mantra, mere number or any other time-unit according to your inclination. Gayatri or OM is the best for Pranayama. In the beginning you must observe some time-unit for Puraka, Kumbhaka and Rechaka. The time-unit and the proper ratio comes by itself when you do the Puraka, Kumbhaka and Rechaka as long as you can do them comfortably. When you have advanced in the practice, you need not count or keep any unit. You will be naturally established in the normal ratio through force of habit.
8. For some days in the beginning you must count the number and see how you progress. In the advanced stages, you need not distract the mind in counting. The lungs will tell you when you have finished the required number.
9. Do not perform the Pranayama till you are fatigued. There must be always joy and exhilaration of spirit during and after the practice. You should come out of the practice fully invigorated and refreshed. Do not bind yourself by too many rules (Niyamas).
10. Do not take bath immediately after Pranayama is over. Take rest for half an hour. If you get perspiration during the practice, do not wipe it with a towel. Rub it with your hand. Do not expose the body to the chill draughts of air when you perspire.
11. Always inhale and exhale very slowly. Do not make any sound. In Pranayamas like Bhastrika and Kapalabhati, you can produce a mild or the lowest possible sound.

12. You should not expect the benefits after doing it for 2 or 3 minutes only for a day or two. At least you must have 15 minutes' daily practice in the beginning regularly for days together. There will be no use if you jump from one exercise to another every day.
13. Patanjali does not lay much stress on the practice of different kinds of Pranayama. He mentions: "Exhale slowly, then inhale and retain the breath. You will get a steady and calm mind." It was only the Hatha Yogins who developed Pranayama as a science and who have mentioned various exercises to suit different persons.
14. A neophyte should do Puraka and Rechaka only without any Kumbhaka for some days. Take a long time to do Rechaka. The proportion for Puraka and Rechaka is 1:2.
15. "Pranayama in its popular and preparatory form may be practised by everyone in any posture whatsoever, sitting or walking; and yet it is sure to show its benefits. For those who practise it in accordance with the prescribed methods, fructification will be rapid."
16. Gradually increase the period of Kumbhaka. Retain for 4 seconds in the first week, for 8 seconds in the second week and for 12 seconds in the third week and so on till you are able to retain the breath to your full capacity.
17. You must so nicely adjust the Puraka, Kumbhaka and Rechaka that you should not experience the feeling of suffocation or discomfort at any stage of Pranayama. You should never feel the necessity of catching hold of a few normal breaths between any two successive rounds. The duration of Puraka, Kumbhaka and Rechaka must be properly adjusted.

Exercise due care and attention. Matters will turn out to be successful and easy.

18. You must not unnecessarily prolong the period of exhalation. If you prolong the time of Rechaka, the following inhalation will be done in a hurried manner and the rhythm will be disturbed. You must so carefully regulate the Puraka, Kumbhaka and Rechaka that you must be able to do with absolute comfort and care, not only of one Pranayama but also the full course or required rounds of Pranayama.

5

IMPORTANCE OF ASANAS

There are four Asanas are prescribed for the purpose of Japa and meditation. They are Padmasana, Siddhasana, Svastikasana and Sukhasana. You must be able to sit in any one of these four Asanas at a stretch for full three hours without shaking the body. Then only you will get Asana-Jaya, mastery over the Asana. Without securing a steady Asana, you cannot further get on well in meditation. The steadier you are in your Asana, the more you will be able to concentrate and make your mind one-pointed. If you can be steady in the posture even for one hour, you will be able to acquire one-pointed mind and feel thereby infinite peace and Atmic Ananda.

When you sit on the posture, think: "I am as firm as a rock". Give this suggestion to the mind half a dozen times. Then the Asana will become steady soon. You must become as a living statue when you sit for Dhyana. Then only there will be real steadiness in your Asana. In one year by regular practice you will have success and will be able to sit for three hours at a stretch. Start with half an hour and gradually increase the period.

When you sit in the Asana, keep your head, neck and trunk in one straight line. Stick to one Asana and make it quite steady and perfect by repeated attempts. Never change the Asana. Adhere to one tenaciously. Realise the full benefits of one Asana. Asana gives Dridhata (strength). Mudra gives Sthirata (steadiness). Pratyahara gives Dhairya (boldness). Pranayama gives Laghima (lightness). Dhyana gives Pratyakshatva (perception) of Self and Samadhi gives Kaivalya (isolation) which is verily the freedom or final beatitude.

In olden days these Asanas were practised in Gurukulas and so the people were strong and healthy and had long lives. In schools and colleges these Asanas should be introduced. Ordinary physical exercises develop the superficial muscles of the body only. One can become a Sandow with a beautiful physique by the physical exercises. But Asanas are intended for physical and spiritual development. These Asanas are useful for concentration, meditation and for awakening the Kundalini.

5.1. PADMASANA

Amongst the four poses prescribed for Japa and Dhyana, Padmasana comes foremost. It is the best Asana for contemplation. Rishis like Gheranda, Sandilya, speak very highly of this vital Asana. This is highly agreeable for householders. Even ladies can sit in this Asana. Padmasana is suitable for lean persons and for youths as well.

Sit on the ground by spreading the legs forward. Then place the right foot on the left thigh and the left foot on the right thigh. Place the hands on the knee-joints. You can make a fingerlock and keep the locked hands over the left ankle. This is very convenient for some persons. Or you can place the left hand over the left knee and then place the right hand over the right knee with the palm facing upwards and the index finger touching the middle portion of the thumb (Chinmudra).

5.2. SIDDHASANA

Next to Padmasana comes Siddhasana in importance. Some eulogise this Asana as even superior to Padmasana for purposes of Dhyana. If you get mastery over this Asana, you will acquire many Siddhis. Further it was being practised by many Siddhas of yore. Hence the name Siddhasana.

Even fatty persons with big thighs can practise this Asana easily. In fact this is better to some persons than Padmasana. Young Brahmacharins who attempt to get established in celibacy should practise this Asana. This Asana is not suitable for ladies. Place one heel at anus. Keep the other heel on the root of the generative organ. The feet or legs should be so nicely arranged that the ankle-joints should touch each other. Hands can be placed as in Padmasana.

5.3. SVASTIKASANA

Svastikasana is sitting at ease with the body erect. Spread the legs forward. Fold the left leg and place the foot near the right thigh muscles. Similarly bend the right leg and push it in the space between the thigh and calf muscles. Now you will find the two feet between the thighs and calves of the legs. This is a very comfortable Asana. Those who find it difficult to do this, can sit in Samasana.

Place the left heel at the beginning of right thigh and the right heel at the beginning of the left thigh. Sit at ease. Do not bend either on the left or right. This is called 'Samasana'.

5.4. SUKHASANA

Any easy, comfortable posture for Japa and meditation is Sukhasana, the important point being the head, neck and trunk should be in a line without curve. People who begin Japa and meditation after 30 or 40 years of age generally are not able to sit in Padma, Siddha or Svastikasana for a long time. People sit in any wrong way and they call it 'Sukhasana'. The trouble is even without their knowledge the backbone forms a curve in a few minutes. Young persons should not try this. This is specially designed to suit old people who are unable to sit in Padmasana or Siddhasana in spite of repeated attempts.

Take a cloth 5 cubits long. Fold it nicely length-wise till the width becomes half a cubit. Sit in your usual way keeping the feet below your thighs. Raise the two knees to the level of your chest till you get a space of 8 or 10 inches between the knees. Now take the folded cloth. Keep one end near the left side, touching the right knee, come to the starting point. Then make a knot of the two ends. Keep your palms face to face and place them on the support of the cloth between the knees. In this Asana the hands, legs and backbone are supported. Hence you will never feel tired. If you cannot do any other Asana sit at least in this Asana and do Japa and meditation for a long time. You can also have Svadhyaya in this Asana.

5.5. SIRSHASANA

Spread a four-folded blanket. Sit on the two knees. Make a finger-lock by interweaving the fingers. Place it on the ground up to the elbow. Now keep the top of your head on this finger-lock or between the two hands. Slowly raise the legs till they become vertical. Stand for five seconds in the beginning and gradually increase the period by 15 seconds each week to 20 minutes or half an hour. Then very slowly, bring it down. Strong people will be able to keep the Asana for half an hour within 2 or 3 months. Do it slowly. There is no harm. If you have time, do twice daily both morning and evening. Perform this

Asana very, very slowly, to avoid jerks. While standing on the head, breathe slowly through the nose and never through the mouth.

You can place the hands on the ground one on each side of the head. You will find this easy to practise, if you are fat. If you have learnt balancing, you can take to the finger-lock method. This Asana is nothing for those who can balance on parallel bars or on the ground. Ask your friend to assist you to keep the legs steady while practising or get the help of a wall. In the beginning some persons may have a novel sensation during practice but this vanishes soon. It brings joy and glee. After the exercise is over take a little rest for five minutes and then take a cup of milk. There are people who are doing this Asana for two or three hours at one stroke.

This is very useful in keeping up Brahmacharya. It makes you Oordhvaretas. The seminal energy is transmuted into spiritual energy, Ojas-Shakti. This is also called sex-sublimation. You will not have wet-dreams, Spermatorrhea. In an Oordhvareto-Yogi the seminal energy flows upwards into the brain for being stored up as spiritual force which is used for contemplative purposes (Dhyana). When you do this Asana, imagine that the seminal energy is being converted into Ojas and is passing along the spinal column into the brain for storage.

Sirshasana is really a blessing and a nectar. Words will fail to adequately describe its beneficial results and effects. In this Asana alone, the brain can draw plenty of Prana and blood. Memory increases admirably. Lawyers, occultists and thinkers will highly appreciate this Asana. This leads to natural Pranayama and Samadhi by itself. No other effort is necessary. If you watch the breath, you will notice it becoming finer and finer. In the beginning of practice there will be a slight difficulty in breathing. As you advance in practice, this vanishes entirely. You will find real pleasure and exhilaration of spirit in this Asana. Great benefit is derived by sitting for meditation after Sirshasana. You can hear Anahata sound quite distinctly. Young, robust persons should perform this Asana. Householders who practise this should not have frequent sexual intercourse.

5.6. SARVANGASANA

This is a mysterious Asana which gives wonderful benefits. Spread a thick blanket on the floor and practise this Asana on the blanket. Lie on the back quite flat. Slowly raise the legs. Lift the trunk, hips, and legs quite vertically. Support the back with the two hands, one on either side. Rest the elbows on the ground. Press the chin against the chest (Jalandhara Bandha). Allow the back-shoulder portion and neck to touch the ground closely. Do not allow the body to shake or move to and fro. Keep the legs straight.

When the Asana is over, bring the legs down very, very slowly with elegance and not with any jerks. In this Asana the whole weight of the body is thrown on the shoulders. You really stand on the shoulders with the help and support of the elbows. Concentrate on the Thyroid gland which lies on the front lower part of the neck. Retain the breath as long as you can do with comfort, and slowly exhale through the nose. You can do this Asana twice daily, morning and evening. This should immediately be followed by Matsyasana (fish-posture). This will relieve pains in the back part of the neck and intensify the usefulness of Sarvangasana. Stand on the Asana for two minutes and gradually increase the period to half an hour.

This is a *panacea*, a cure-all, a sovereign specific for all diseases. It brightens the psychic faculties and awakens Kundalini Sakti, removes all sorts of diseases of intestine and stomach, and augments the mental power.

It supplies a large quantity of blood to the roots of spinal nerves. It is this Asana which centralises the blood in the spinal column and nourishes it beautifully. But for this Asana there is no scope for these nerve-roots to draw sufficient blood-supply. It keeps the spine quite elastic. Elasticity of the spine means everlasting youth. It stimulates you in your work. It prevents the spine from early ossification (hardening). So you will preserve and retain your youth for a long time. It helps a lot in maintaining Brahmacharya. Like Sirshasana, it makes you an Oordhvaretas. It checks wet-dreams effectively.

It rejuvenates those who have lost their potency. It acts as a powerful blood-tonic and purifier. It tones the nerves and awakens Kundalini. Spinal column is rendered very soft and elastic. This Asana prevents the early ossification of the vertebral bones. Ossification is quick degeneration of bones. Old age manifests quickly on account of early ossification. The bones become hard and brittle in the degenerative process. He who practises Sarvangasana is very nimble, agile, full of energy. The muscles of the back are alternately contracted, relaxed and then pulled and stretched. Hence they draw a good supply of blood by these various movements and are well nourished. Various sorts of myalgia (muscular rheumatism), lumbago, sprain, neuralgia, etc., are cured by this Asana.

The vertebral column becomes as soft and elastic as rubber. It is twisted and rolled as it were like a piece of canvas sheet. A man who practises this Asana can never become lazy even a bit. He is a two-legged talking squirrel. The vertebral column is a very important structure. It supports the whole body. It contains the spinal cord, spinal nerve and sympathetic system. In Hatha Yoga the spine is termed as Meru Danda. Therefore you must keep it healthy, strong and elastic. The muscles of the abdomen, the rectic muscles and the muscles of the thigh are also toned and nourished well. Obesity or corpulence and habitual chronic constipation, Gulma, congestion and enlargement of the liver and spleen are cured by this Asana.

5.7. MATSYASANA

This Asana will help one to float on water easily with Plavini Pranayama. Therefore it is called fish-pose, Matsyasana. Spread a blanket and sit on Padmasana by keeping the right foot over the left thigh and the left over right thigh. Then lie flat on the back. Hold the head by the two elbows. This is one variety.

Stretch the head back, so that the top of your head rests on the ground firmly on one side and the buttocks only on the other, thus making a bridge or an arch of the trunk. Place the hands on the thighs or catch the toes with the hands. You will have to give a good twisting to the back. This variety is more efficacious than the former one. The benefits that you derive from this variety are a hundred times more than what you get in the previous variety.

Those fatty persons with thick calves, who find it difficult to have Padmasaṇa (foot-lock), may simply sit in the ordinary way and then practise this Asana. Practise the Padmasana first. Make it firm, easy and steady. Then take Matsyasana. Do this Asana for 10 seconds in the beginning and increase it to 10 minutes. When you have finished the Asana, slowly release the head with the help of hands and get up. Then unlock the Padmasana.

You must practise this Asana soon after Sarvangasana. It will relieve stiffness of the neck and all crampy conditions of the cervical region caused by long practice of Sarvangasana. This gives natural massage or shampooing to the congested parts of the neck and shoulders. Further it affords the maximum benefits of

Sarvangasana. It is a complimentary Asana of Sarvangasana. Rather it supplements Sarvangasana. As the larynx or wind-box and trachea (wind-pipe) are thrown open widely, this Asana helps deep breathing.

Matsyasana is the destroyer of many diseases. It removes constipation. It brings down the accumulated faecal matter to the rectum. It is useful in asthma, consumption, chronic bronchitis, etc., on account of the deep breathing.

5.8. PASCHIMOTTANASANA

Sit on the ground and stretch the legs stiff like a stick. Catch the toes with the thumb and index and middle fingers. While catching, you have to bend the trunk forwards. Fatty persons will find it rather difficult to bend. Exhale. Slowly bend without jerks till your forehead touches your knees. You can keep the face even between the knees. When you bend down, draw the belly back. This facilitates the bending forward. Bend slowly by gradual degrees. Take your own time. There is no hurry. When you bend down, bend the head between the hands. Retain it on a level with them. Young persons with elastic spine can touch the knees with the forehead even in their very first attempt. In the case of grown-up persons with rigid spinal column, it will take a fortnight or a month for complete success in the posture. Retain the breath till you take the forehead back, to its original position, till you sit straight again. Then breathe.

Retain the pose for 5 seconds. Then gradually increase the period to 10 minutes.

Those who find it difficult to do the full Paschimottanasana, can do half pose with one leg and one hand and then with the other leg and hand. They will find this more easy. After some days when the spine has become more elastic, they can have recourse to the full pose. You will have to use common-sense while practising Yogasanas.

This is an excellent Asana. It makes the breath flow through the Brahma Nadi and Sushumna, and rouses the gastric fire. It reduces fat in the abdomen and makes the loins lean. This Asana is a specific for corpulence or obesity. It brings about reduction of spleen and liver in cases of enlargement of spleen. What Sarvangasana is for the stimulation of endocrine glands, so is Paschimottanasana for the stimulation of abdominal viscera, such as kidneys, liver, pancreas, etc.

This Asana relieves constipation, removes sluggishness of liver, dyspepsia, belching and gastritis. Lumbago and all sorts of myalgia of the back muscles are cured. This Asana cures piles and diabetes also. The muscles of the abdomen, the solar plexus, the epigastric plexus, bladder prostate, lumbar nerves, sympathetic cord are all toned up and kept in a healthy, sound condition.

5.9. MAYURASANA

This is more difficult than Sarvangasana. This demands good physical strength. Kneel on the ground. Sit on the toes. Raise the heels up. Join the two forearms together. Place the palms of the two hands on the ground. The two little fingers must be in close touch. They project towards the feet. Now you have got steady and firm forearms for supporting the whole body in the ensuing elevation of the trunk and legs. Now bring down the abdomen slowly against the conjoined elbows. Support your body upon your elbows that are pressed now against the navel or umbilicus. This is the first stage. Stretch your legs and raise the feet stiff and straight on a level with the head. This is second stage.

Neophytes (beginners) find it difficult to keep up the balance as soon as they raise the feet from the ground.

Place a cushion in front. Sometimes you will have a fall forwards and you may hurt your nose slightly. Try to slip on the sides when you cannot keep up the balance. If you find it difficult to stretch the two legs backwards at one stroke, slowly stretch one leg first and then the other. If you adopt the device of leaning the body forwards and head downwards the feet will by themselves leave the ground and you can stretch them quite easily. When the Asana is in full manifestation the head, trunk, buttocks, thighs, legs and feet will be in one straight line and parallel to the ground. This posture is very beautiful to look at.

Beginners can practise this Asana by holding on to a table. They will find it easy to practise this. If you understand the technique of this Asana and if you use your common-sense you can do it easily and can keep up the balance without much difficulty. Fatty people have frequent nasty falls, slips and doublings and they excite much laughter amongst the onlookers. Do not bend the legs when you stretch them.

Practise this Asana from 5 to 20 seconds. Those who have good physical strength can do it for 2 or 3 minutes. Retain the breath when you raise the body. It will give you immense strength. When you finish the Asana, exhale slowly.

This is a wonderful Asana for improving digestion. It destroys the effects of unwholesome food, and increases the digestive power. It cures dyspepsia and diseases of the stomach like Gulma (chronic gastritis), and reduces spleenic and liver enlargements by increasing the intra-abdominal pressure. The whole abdominal organs are properly toned and stimulated well by the increase of intra-abdominal pressure. Sluggishness of liver or hepatic torpidity disappears. It tones the bowels and removes constipation (ordinary, chronic and habitual). It awakens Kundalini.

5.10. ARDHA MATSYENDRASANA

Paschimottanasana and Halasana bend the spine forwards. Dhanur, Bhujanga and Salabha Asanas are counter-poses to bend the spine backwards. This is not sufficient. It must be twisted and bent from side to side also (lateral movements). Then only perfect elasticity of the spinal column can be ensured. The Matsyendrasana serves this purpose well in giving a lateral twist to the spinal column.

Place the left heel near the anus and below the scrotum. It can touch the perennial space. Do not allow the heel to move from this space. Bend the knee and place the right ankle at the root of the left thigh and rest the right foot well on the ground close to the left hip-joint. Place the left *axilla* or arm-pit over the top of the vertically bent right knee. Push the knee now a little to the back so that it touches the back part of the *axilla*. Catch hold of the left foot with left palm. Then applying pressure at the left shoulder-joint slowly twist the spine and turn to the extreme right. Turn the face also to the right as much as you can do. Bring it in a line with the right shoulder. Swing round the right arm towards the back. Catch hold of the left thigh with the right hand. Retain the pose from 5 to 15 seconds. Keep the vertebral column erect. Do not bend. Similarly you can twist the spine to the left side.

This Asana increases appetite by increasing the digestive fire. It destroys terrible diseases. It rouses Kundalini and makes the moon-flow, Chandranadi, steady. Above the root of the palate the moon is said to be located. It drops the cool ambrosial nectar, which is wasted by mixing with gastric fire. But this Asana prevents it. It keeps the spine elastic and gives a good massage to the abdominal organs. Lumbago and all sorts of muscular rheumatism of the back-muscles are cured.

The spinal nerve-roots and sympathetic system are toned. They draw a good supply of blood. This Asana is an adjunct to Paschimottanasana.

5.11. VAJRASANA

Those who sit in this Asana have a quite steady and firm pose. They cannot be easily shaken. The knees are rendered very hard. Merudanda becomes firm and strong. This Asana resembles more or less the Namaz pose in which the Muslims sit for prayer.

Keep the soles of the feet on both sides of the anus, i.e., place the thighs on the legs one over the other and the soles on the buttocks. The calves must touch the thighs. The part from the toe to the knee should touch the ground. The whole burden of the body is put on the knees and ankles. In the beginning of practice you may feel a slight pain in the knee and ankle-joints but it passes off very quickly.

Massage the painful parts and two joints with the hands. You can use a little Iodex or Amrutanjan for rubbing. After fixing the feet and the knees, put both the hands straight on the knees. Keep the knees quite close. Sit like this keeping the trunk, neck and head in one straight line. This is the most common Asana. You can sit in this Asana for a very long time comfortably. Yogins generally sit in this Asana.

If you sit in this Asana for fifteen minutes immediately after food, the food will be digested well. Dyspeptics will derive much benefit. The Nadis, nerves and muscles of the legs and thighs are strengthened. Myalgia in the knees, legs, toes and thighs disappears. Sciatica vanishes. Flatulence is removed. Stomach exercises a stimulating, beneficial influence on Kanda, the most vital part from which all the Nadis spring.

5.12. URDHVA PADMASANA

Perform Sirshasana. Slowly bend the right leg and keep it on the left thigh and keep the left leg on the right thigh. You must do this very carefully and slowly. If you can stand in Sirshasana for more than 10 or 15 minutes, then you can attempt this. Otherwise you will have a fall and injure your legs. A gymnast, who can balance on the parallel bars on the ground, can do this. The benefits of Sirshasana can be realised from this Asana.

6

IMPORTANCE OF MUDRAS AND BANDHAS

Mudras and Bandhas are certain postures of the body by which Kundalini is successfully awakened. In Gheranda Samhita, the description of 25 Mudras and Bandhas, is given. The following 12 are the most important:—

1. Mula Bandha
2. Jalandhara Bandha
3. Uddiyana Bandha
4. Maha Mudra
5. Maha Bandha
6. Maha Vedha
7. Yoga Mudra
8. Viparitakarani Mudra
9. Khechari Mudra
10. Vajroli Mudra
11. Shakti Chalana Mudra
12. Yoni Mudra

Many aspirants are not able to find out the exact technique of several Mudras that are described in Hatha

Yogic texts, and therefore they could not realise the benefits. Yogic exercises when practised regularly in the right way, will surely bestow on you all that you want. Dyspepsia, constipation, piles, cough, asthma, enlargement of spleen, venereal diseases, leprosy and all sorts of incurable diseases are cured by Mudras and Bandhas. They are the most effective exercises for maintaining Brahmacharya, without which nothing can be made in the spiritual path.

6.1. MULA BANDHA

Press the Yoni with the left heel. Keep the right heel pressed at the space just above the organ of generation. Contract the anus and draw the Apana Vayu upwards. This is called Mula Bandha. The Apana Vayu which does the function of ejection of excreta has natural tendency to move downwards. Through the practice of Mula Bandha, the Apana Vayu is made to move upwards by contracting the anus and by forcibly drawing it upwards. The Prana Vayu is united with the Apana and the united Prana-Apana Vayu is made to enter the Sushumna Nadi.

Then the Yogi attains perfection in Yoga. Kundalini is awakened. The Yogi drinks the Nectar of Immortality. He enjoys Siva-pada in Sahasrara Chakra. He gets all divine Vibhutis and Aishvarya. When the Apana is united with Prana, Anahata sounds (mystical inner sounds) are heard very distinctly. Prana, Apana, Nada and Bindu unite and the Yogi reaches perfection in Yoga. This highest stage cannot be reached by the first attempt. One should practise this again and again for a long time.

The Siddhi in the practice of Pranayama is attained through the help of Bandhas and Mudras. The practice of Mula Bandha enables one to keep up perfect Brahmacharya, gives Dhatu-Pushti (nerve-vigour), relieves constipation and increases Jatharagni. During the practice of concentration, meditation, Pranayama and all other Yogic Kriyas, Mula Bandha can be combined.

6.2. JALANDHARA BANDHA

Contract the throat. Press the chin firmly against the chest. This Bandha is practised at the end of Puraka and beginning of Kumbhaka. Generally this Bandha is done during Kumbhaka only. The gastric fire, which is situated in the region of Nabhi, consumes the nectar which exudes out of the Sahasrara Chakra through the hole in the palate. This Bandha prevents the nectar being thus consumed.

6.3. UDDIYANA BANDHA

The Sanskrit word "Uddiyana" comes from the root 'ut' and 'di' which means to "fly up." When this Bandha is practised the Prana flies up through the Sushumna Nadi. Hence the significant name.

Empty the lungs by a strong and forcible expiration. The lungs will become completely empty when you exhale forcibly through the mouth. Now contract and draw up the intestines above and below the navel towards the back, so that the abdomen rests against the back of the body high up in the thoracic cavity. This is Uddiyana Bandha. This is practised at the end of Kumbhaka and beginning of the Rechaka. When you practise this Bandha, the diaphragm, the muscular portion between the thoracic cavity and abdomen, is raised up and the abdominal muscles are drawn backwards. If you bend your trunk forwards, you can easily do this exercise. Uddiyana Bandha is the first stage of Nauli Kriya. You should know Uddiyana Bandha if you want to practise Nauli Kriya. Nauli Kriya is generally done in a standing position. Uddiyana Bandha can be practised in a sitting or standing posture. When you do it while standing, keep your hands on the thigh as shown in the illustration.

This exercise helps a lot in keeping up Brahmacharya. It imparts beautiful health, strength, vigour and vitality to the practitioner. When it is combined with Nauli Kriya, it serves as a powerful gastro-intestinal tonic. These are the two potent weapons of the Yogin to combat against constipation, weak peristalsis of the intestines and other disorders of the alimentary canal. It is by these two Yogic Kriyas alone, that you can manipulate and massage all the abdominal muscles.

For abdominal exercises nothing can compete with Uddiyana Bandha and Nauli. They stand unique and unrivalled amongst all systems of physical exercises. In chronic diseases of stomach and intestines, where drugs of all sorts have failed, Uddiyana and Nauli have effected a rapid, thorough and marvellous cure. When you practise Pranayama, you can beautifully combine Mula Bandha, Jalandhara Bandha and Uddiyana Bandha. This is Bandha-Traya.

Uddiyana Bandha reduces fat in the belly. In cases where Marienbud reduction pills have failed to reduce fat, Uddiyana Bandha will work wonders. If fatty persons stop taking ghee and reduce the quantity of drinking water, they will be able to do Uddiyana. A trip to Kedar-Badri or Mount Kailas by foot will prepare fatty people for the practice of Uddiyana Bandha.

6.4. MAHA MUDRA

This is the most important of all Mudras. Hence it is called 'Maha Mudra.' Press the anus carefully with the left heel. Stretch out the right leg. Catch hold of the toe with the two hands. Inhale and retain the breath. Press the chin against the chest firmly (Jalandhara Bandha). Fix the gaze between the eyebrows (Bhrumadhya Drishti).

Retain the posture as long as you can and then exhale slowly. Practise first on the left leg and then on the right leg.

This cures consumption, haemorrhoids or piles, enlargement of spleen, indigestion, Gulma (chronic gastritis), leprosy, constipation, fever and all other diseases. Life is increased. It confers great Siddhis on the practitioners. Generally the Yogi does Maha Mudra, Maha Bandha and Maha Vedha. This is a good combination. Then only maximum benefits are derived. Do like this six times in the morning and evening.

6.5. MAHA BANDHA

Maha Mudra is the preliminary exercise for this. Press the anus with the left heel. Place the right foot upon the left thigh. Contract the anus and muscles of the perineum. Draw the Apana Vayu upwards. Draw the breath slowly and retain it by Jalandhara Bandha as long as you can. Then exhale slowly. Practise first on the left side and then on the right side. The Bandha destroys decay and death. The Yogi achieves all his desires and obtains Siddhis.

6.6. MAHA VEDHA

Sit in Maha Bandha posture. Draw the breath slowly. Retain the breath. Press the chin against the chest. Place the palms on the ground. Rest the body on the palms. Raise the buttocks slowly and strike them gently against the ground. The Asana must be intact and firm when you raise the buttocks. This Kriya destroys decay and death. The Yogi gets control over the mind and conquers death. There is not much difference between Maha Mudra, Maha Bandha and Maha Vedha. They are something like 3 stages of one exercise.

6.7. YOGA MUDRA

Sit in Padmasana. Place the palms on the heels. Exhale slowly and bend forwards and touch the ground with the forehead. If you retain the pose for a long time, you can breathe as usual. Or come to the former position and inhale. Instead of keeping the hands on the heels, you can take them to the back. Catch hold of the left wrist with your right hand. This pose removes all kinds of disorders of the abdomen.

6.8. VIPARITAKARANI MUDRA

Lie on the ground. Raise the legs up straight. Support the buttocks with the hands. Rest the elbows on the ground. Remain steady. The sun dwells at the root of the navel and the moon at the root of the palate. The process by which the sun is brought upward and the moon is carried downward is called Viparitakarani Mudra. The positions of the sun and the moon are reversed. On the first day do it for a minute. Gradually increase the period to three hours. After six months wrinkles on the face and grey hair disappear. The Yogin who practises this for three hours daily conquers death. As the gastric fire is increased, those who practise this Mudra for a long time should take some light refreshment such as milk, etc., as soon as the Kriya is over. Sirshasana posture also is called Viparitakarani Mudra.

6.9. KHECHARI MUDRA

'Kha' means Akasa and 'Chari' means to move. The Yogi moves in the Akasa. The tongue and the mind remain in the Akasa. Hence this is known as Khechari Mudra.

This Mudra can be performed by a man, only if he has undergone the preliminary exercise under the direct guidance of a Guru, who is practising Khechari Mudra.

The preliminary portion of this Mudra is in making the tongue so long that the tip of the tongue might touch the space between the two eyebrows. The Guru will cut the lower tendon of the tongue with a bright, clean knife little by little every week. By sprinkling salt and turmeric powder, the cut edges may not join together again. Cutting the lower tendon of the tongue should be done regularly, once a week, for a period of six months. Rub the tongue with fresh butter and draw it out. Take hold of the tongue with the fingers and move it to and fro. Milking the tongue means taking hold of it and drawing it as the milkman does the udder of a cow during milking. By all these means you can lengthen the tongue to reach the forehead. This is the preliminary portion of Khechari Mudra. Then turn the tongue upwards and backwards by sitting in Siddhasana so as to touch the palate and close the posterior nasal openings with the reversed tongue and fix the gaze on the space between the two eye-brows. Now leaving the Ida and Pingala, Prana will move in the Sushumna Nadi. The respiration will stop. The tongue is on the mouth of the well of nectar. This is Khechari Mudra.

By the practice of this Mudra the Yogi is free from fainting, hunger, thirst and laziness. He is free from diseases, decay, old age and death. This Mudra makes one an Oordhvaretas. As the body of the Yogi is filled with nectar, he will not die even by virulent poison. This Mudra gives Siddhis to Yogins. Khechari is the best of all Mudras.

But never try doing this all. The simplest way is to turn the tongue upwards and just touch the palate.

6.10. VAJROLI MUDRA

This is an important Yogic Kriya in Hatha Yoga. You will have to work hard to get full success in this Kriya. There are very few people who are experts in this act. Yogic students draw water first through a silver-tube (catheter specially made) passed into the urethra 12 inches inside. After due practice they draw milk, then oil, honey, etc. They draw mercury in the end. Later on they can draw these liquids directly through the urethra without the help of the silver-tube. This Kriya is of immense use for keeping up perfect Brahmacharya. On the first day you should send the catheter inside the urethra for one inch only, the second day two inches, third day three inches, and so on. You must gradually practise till you are able to send 12 inches of the catheter inside. The way becomes clear and blowing. Raja Bhartrihari could do this Kriya very dexterously.

Even a drop of semen cannot come out of the Yogi who practises this Mudra. Even if it is discharged, he can draw it back through this Mudra. The Yogi, who draws his semen up and preserves it, conquers death. Good smell emanates from his body. The late Trilingaswami of Varanasi was an expert in this Kriya. Sri Swami Kuvalayanandaji of Lonavala teaches this Mudra. Some persons call the Mayurasana Vajroli Mudra. Again Vajroli Mudra is also known as Yoni Mudra. However, the description of Yoni Mudra is given separately.

The object of Vajroli Mudra is to be perfectly established in Brahmacharya. When aspirants practise this Mudra, they unconsciously divert their mind to sexual centres and thereby they cannot get any success. When you see the description of this Mudra, you will clearly understand that strict Brahmacharya is absolutely necessary. For practising this there is no necessity at all for a woman or for any sexual intercourse. Since the Grihasthas have their wives and because they think that Vajroli Mudra is a device for birth-control, they have a keen desire to practise this Mudra. It is all mere foolishness and delusion. They have not understood the technique and object of this important Kriya. Practice of Mula Bandha, Maha Bandha, Maha Mudra, Asanas, Pranayamas, etc., will naturally enable one to understand and to get success in the practice of Vajroli. This must be done under the direct guidance of a Guru.

6.11. SHAKTI CHALANA MUDRA

Sit in a secluded room in Siddhasana. Draw in the air forcibly and join it with Apana. Do Mula Bandha till the Vayu enters the Sushumna. By retaining the air, the Kundalini, feeling suffocated, awakes and finds its way through Sushumna to Brahmarandhra. Sit in Siddhasana. Take hold of the foot near the ankle and slowly beat the Kanda with the foot. This is Tadana Kriya. By this method also Kundalini can be awakened. Through the practice of this Mudra one can become a Siddha.

6.12. YONI MUDRA

Sit in Siddhasana. Close the ears with the two thumbs, eyes with the index-fingers, nostrils with the middle-fingers, the upper lips with the ring-fingers and the lower lips with the little fingers. This is a beautiful pose for doing Japa. Dive deep and meditate on the Shat Chakras and Kundalini. This is not quite easy for all like other Mudras. You have to exert much in getting success in this. You must be perfectly established in Brahmacharya if you want sure success. "*Devanamapi durlabha*"—very difficult to be obtained even by Devas. Therefore realise the importance of this Mudra and practise it very cautiously. Vajroli Mudra also is called Yoni Mudra.

6.13. LAYA YOGA

Laya is the state of mind when one forgets all the objects of senses and gets absorbed in the object of meditation.

Laya enables one to have perfect control over the five Tattvas, mind and Indriyas. The fluctuations of mind will stop. The mind, body and Prana will be entirely subdued.

For Laya Yoga, Sambhavi Mudra is an effective method, in which one intently concentrates on any one of the Shat Chakras. Trataka exercise plays a vital part in getting success in Laya. In due course of practice, the Yogin gets established in Samadhi. He becomes a Jivanmukta.

6.14. ANAHATA SOUNDS

Anahata sounds are the mystic sounds heard by the Yogin during his meditation. It is a sign of the purification of Nadis. Some students can clearly hear it through any one of the ears and some by both the ears. There are loud as well as subtle sounds. From the loud, one will have to contemplate on the subtle and from the subtle to the subtler. Beginners can hear the sound only when the ears are closed. Advanced students can concentrate on the Anahata sound even without closing the ears. Anahata sound is also termed Omkara Dhvani. They proceed from the Anahata centre of the Sushumna Nadi.

Sit in your usual Asana. Close the ears with the thumbs. Hear and minutely observe the internal sound through the ears. The sound that you hear from within will make you deaf to all external sounds. Close the eyes also. In the beginning of your practice, you will hear many loud sounds. Later on they are heard in a mild way. The mind having at first concentrated itself on any one sound fixes firmly to that and is absorbed in it. The mind becoming insensible to the external impressions, becomes one with the sound as milk with water and then becomes rapidly absorbed in Chidakasa.

Just as the bee drinking the honey alone does not care for the odour so also the Chitta, which is always absorbed in the inner sound, does not long for sensual objects, as it is bound by the sweet smell or Nada and has abandoned its flitting nature.

The sound proceeding from Pranava Nada, which is Brahman, is of the nature of effulgence. The mind gets absorbed in it. The mind exists so long as there is sound, but with its cessation, there is that state termed Turiya. It is the supreme state. It is the Unmani state. The mind gets absorbed along with Prana by constant concentration upon Nada. The body appears to be a log of wood and it does not feel heat or cold, joy or sorrow. Different kinds of sounds proceed from the heart (Anahata sounds).

Nada that is heard through the ears is of ten kinds. The first is the sound *'Chini'* (like the pronunciation of the word); the second is *'Chini-chini'*; the third is the sound of a bell; the fourth is that of a conch; the fifth is that of a lute; the sixth is the sound of cymbals; the seventh is the tune of a flute; the eighth is the voice of a drum (Bheri); the ninth is the sound of a double-drum (Mridanga); and the tenth is the sound of thunder.

You cannot expect the sound immediately after you close your ears. You should concentrate and keep your mind one-pointed. The particular sound that you hear today, you may not hear every day. But you will hear any one of the ten Anahata sounds.

The description given above is Laya through Nada, Anahata sound. In the same manner, Laya can be effected by concentration at the tip of the nose (Nasikagra Drishti), at the space between the two eyebrows (Bhrumadhya Drishti), meditation on the five Tattvas, on Soham Mantra, Aham Brahma Asmi, Tat Tvam Asi Mahavakyas and other methods also.

6.15. BHAKTI YOGA

At the lowest rung of the ladder of Bhakti Yoga comes the worship of elements and departed spirits. This is the lowest form of worship. Next comes the worship of Rishis, Devas and Pitris. The faith of each is shaped according to his own nature. The man consists of that which his faith is, he is even that. The third class includes those followers who worship Avataras like Sri Rama, Krishna, Narasimha. The above four classes of Bhaktas have the Saguna form of worship. Next comes the class of Bhaktas who do Nirguna Upasana on Brahman devoid of attributes. This is the highest form of worship that is suitable for the intelligent people who have strong will and bold understanding. This is known as Ahamgraha Upasana or Jnana Yoga Sadhana.

Bhakti can be acquired and cultivated. Practice of the Nava Vidha Bhakti (nine methods of devotion) will infuse Bhakti. Constant Satsanga, Japa, Prayer, meditation, Svadhyaya, Bhajan, service to saints, Dana, Yatra, etc., will develop Bhakti. The following are the nine methods of developing Bhakti:

1. Sravana:—hearing of the Lilas of God
2. Smarana:—remembering God always
3. Kirtan:—singing His praise
4. Vandana:—Namaskaras to God
5. Archana:—offerings to God
6. Pada-Sevana:—attendance
7. Sakhya:—friendship
8. Dasya:—service

6.16. MANTRAS

Awakening Kundalini is effected by Mantra also. It is a

portion of Bhakti Yoga. Some aspirants should repeat the Mantra given by their Guru even lakhs of times. During the time of Diksha of an Uttama Adhikari, the Guru utters a particular Mantra and Kundalini is awakened immediately. The consciousness of the student is raised to a very high degree. This depends upon the faith of the student in his Guru and in the Mantra.

Mantras, when received from the Guru in person, are very powerful. Aspirants in Kundalini Yoga should take to this Mantra Sadhana only after getting a proper Mantra from a Guru.

6.17. SIDDHIS

An accomplished, Purnayogi in the path of Kundalini Yoga is in possession of eight major Siddhis, viz., Anima, Mahima, Laghima, Garima, Prapti, Prakamya, Vasitvam and Ishitvam.

1. *Anima*: The Yogi can become as minute as he pleases.
2. *Mahima*: This is the opposite of Anima. He can become as big as he likes. He can make his body assume a very large size. He can fill up the whole universe. He can assume a Virat Svarupa.
3. *Laghima*: He can make his body as light as cotton or feather. Vayustambhanam is done through this Siddhi. In Jalastambhanam also the power is exercised to a very small degree. The body is rendered light by Plavini Pranayama. The Yogi produces a diminution of his specific gravity by swallowing large draughts of air. The Yogi travels in the sky with the help of this Siddhi. He can travel thousands of miles in a minute.
4. *Garima*: This is the opposite of Laghima. In this the Yogi acquires an increase of specific gravity. He can

make the body as heavy as a mountain by swallowing draughts of air.

5. *Prapti*: The Yogi standing on the earth can touch the highest things. He can touch the sun or the moon or the sky. Through this Siddhi the Yogi attains his desired objects and supernatural powers. He acquires the power of predicting future events, the power of clairvoyance, clairaudience, telepathy, thought-reading, etc. He can understand the languages of the beasts and birds. He can understand unknown languages also. He can cure all diseases.
6. *Prakamya*: He can dive into the water and can come out at any time he likes. The late Trilinga Swami of Benares used to live for six months underneath the Ganges. It is the process by which a Yogi makes himself invisible sometimes. By some writers it is defined to be the power of entering body of another (Parakaya Pravesh). Sri Sankara entered the body of Raja Amaruka of Benares. Tirumular in Southern India entered the body of a shepherd. Raja Vikramaditya also did this. It is also the power of keeping a youth-like appearance for any length of time. Raja Yayati had this power.
7. *Vashitvam*: This is the power of taming wild animals and bringing them under control. It is the power of mesmerising persons by the exercise of will and of making them obedient to one's own wishes and orders. It is the restraint of passions and emotions. It is the power to bring men, women and the elements under subjection.
8. *Ishitvam*: It is the attainment of divine power. The Yogi becomes the Lord of the universe. The Yogi who has this power can restore life to the dead. Kabir, Tulsidas, Akalkot Swami and others had this power of bringing back life to the dead.

The Yogi acquires the following minor Siddhis also:

1. Freedom from hunger and thirst.
2. Freedom from the effects of heat and cold.
3. Freedom from Raga-Dvesha.
4. Doora Darshan, clairvoyance or Dooradrishti.
5. Doora Sravan, clairaudience or Doora Sruti and Doora Pravachana.
6. Mano-Jaya, control of mind.
7. Kama Rupa: The Yogi can take any form he likes.
8. Parakaya Pravesha: He can enter into another body, can animate a dead body and enter into it by transferring his soul.
9. Iccha-Mrityu: Death at his will.
10. Devanam Saha Kreeda and Darshana: Playing with the gods after seeing them.
11. Yatha Sankalpa: Can get whatever he likes.
12. Trikala-Jnana: Knowledge of past, present and future.
13. Advandva: Beyond the pairs of opposites.
14. Vak-Siddhi: Whatever the Yogi predicts will come to pass by the practice of Satya, Prophecy.
15. The Yogi can turn base metal into gold.
16. Kaya-Vyuha: Taking as many bodies as the Yogi likes to exhaust all his Karmas in one life.
17. Darduri-Siddhi: The jumping power of a frog.
18. Patala-Siddhi: Yogi becomes Lord of desire, destroys sorrows and diseases.
19. He gets knowledge of his past life.
20. He gets knowledge of the cluster of stars and planets.

21. He gets the power of perceiving the Siddhas.
22. He gets mastery of the elements (Bhuta Jaya), mastery of Prana (Prana Jaya).
23. Kamachari: He can move to any place he likes.
24. He gets omnipotence and omniscience.
25. Vayu-Siddhi: The Yogi rises in the air and leaves the ground.
26. He can point out the place where a hidden treasure lies.

A Yogi forgets the body in order to concentrate the mind on the Lord. He conquers heat and cold by mastering breath-control and by controlling his nervous system.

A Yogi generates psychic heat in the body through the practice of Bhastrika Pranayama.

He can bear extremes of climates without discomfort.

He sits on the snow and melts it by the warmth generated in his body.

A Yogi covers his body with a sheet dipped in very cold water and dries it by the Yoga heat given off from his body. A few adepts have dried as many as thirty sheets in a single night.

A perfect Yogi cremates his body in the end by the Yogic heat generated by his power of Yoga.

7

CHAKRAS: THE TRANSFORMATION TOOLS

The chakras are the ancient depositories of all the divine energy given to humanity at the beginning of time. They are "The seven Spirits" guiding us on our path of transformation, our initiation into the mysteries of life. The knowledge and use of chakras as a means to spiritual awakening has been recognised through the ages in all the great religions in one form or another. These powerful tools for transformation have become in our time a focus of great interest and fascination.

The famous psychologist Carl Jung called the chakras the "gateways of consciousness". They are connected to our thinking, feeling and willing through our breath, through our etheric body, through our voice and through movement and our consciousness is developed and shaped by the dominant energy of our lower or higher chakras.

As long as we are not aware of our chakras, they operate on a subconscious level. If a person has no concept whatsoever of anything beyond the material level the chakras can be said to be dormant, they hardly rotate at all. When we start to question who we are, what our purpose is, and begin to consciously develop our divine nature, the chakras quicken, become active and our spiritual mind, heart and will start to develop.

Inside every human being there is a network of nerves and sensory organs that interprets the outside physical world. At the same time, within us resides a subtle system of channels (nadis) and centers of energy (chakras) which look after our physical, intellectual, emotional and spiritual being.

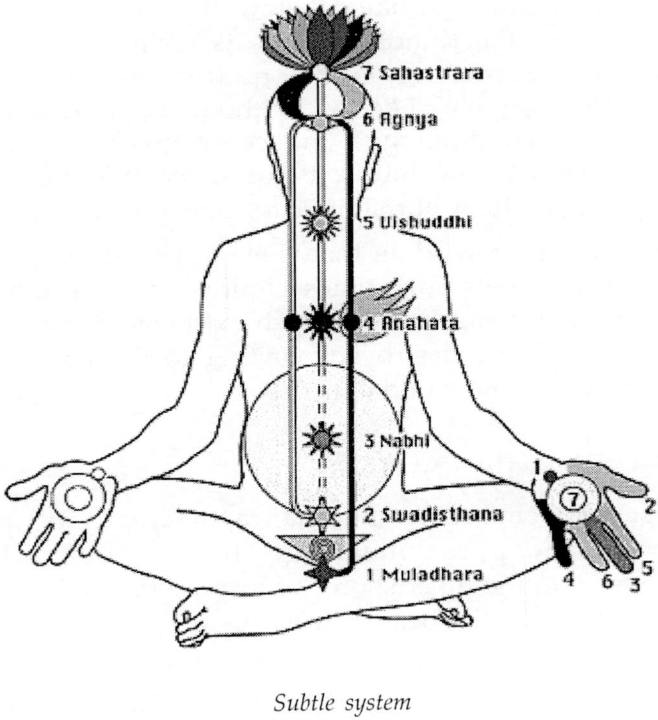

Subtle system

Each of the seven chakras has several spiritual qualities. These qualities are intact within us, and even though they might not always be manifest, they can never be destroyed. When the Kundalini is awakened, these qualities start manifesting spontaneously and express themselves in our life. Thus, through regular meditation, we become automatically very dynamic, creative, confident and at the same time very humble, loving and compassionate. It is a process which starts to develop by itself when the Kundalini rises and starts to nourish our chakras.

7.1. MOOLADHARA CHAKRA

The first chakra is situated below the sacrum bone in which resides the Kundalini, and its main aspect is the innocence. Innocence is the quality by which we experience pure, childlike joy, without the limitations of prejudice or conditionings. Innocence gives us dignity, balance, and a tremendous sense of direction and purpose in life. It is nothing but simplicity, purity and joy.

It is the inner wisdom that is ever present in the little children, and gets sometimes clouded by our modern lifestyles. But it is a quality which exists eternally within us and cannot be destroyed, waiting to be manifest as pure joy when the Kundalini rises.

7.2. SWADISHTHAN CHAKRA

The second chakra is the chakra of creativity, pure attention and pure knowledge. It is the one which connects us to the inner source of inspiration, and enables us to experience the beauty around us.

The pure knowledge given by this chakra is not mental, but it is direct perception of the Reality, that can be felt in our palms and indicates our subtle blockages. Also this is the center of pure, steady attention and power of concentration.

On the physical level it looks after our liver, kidneys, and the lower abdomen. When we think too much, this center gets drained of energy and diseases like diabetes or blood cancer can occur when this chakra goes completely out of balance.

7.3. MANIPUR CHAKRA

The third chakra is the one that gives us the sense of generosity, complete satisfaction and contentment.

On the left side, the main quality of this center is peace—clearing this chakra can relieve stress and tensions.

On the right side, it looks after our liver which is the organ of our attention and power of concentration.

When enlightened by the Kundalini, the Manipur chakra gives us our spiritual ascent, righteousness and inner sense of morality, and complete balance at all levels in our life.

7.3.1. The Void

Surrounding the second and the third chakra is the Void which stands for the principle of mastery (guru principle) within us.

In many spiritual traditions, this area is the "ocean of illusions" that needs to be crossed with the help of a spiritual guide. When the Kundalini is awakened and passes through the Void, this principle of mastery is established within us.

Thus, as Shri Mataji says, in Sahaja Yoga you become your own guru, your own spiritual guide since you can feel on your fingertips all your subtle problems and have the power to cure them using your own Kundalini.

Moreover, establishing this center helps us get rid of all our habits, laziness, gross attachments, and everything that enslaves us in a way or another: we become our own master.

Following false "gurus" who are more interested in power tricks or your purse can damage very much the Void area. But after Self Realisation, everything can be cured through the purifying power of the Kundalini in meditation.

7.4. THE HEART CHAKRA OR ANAHAT CHAKRA

The fourth chakra, the chakra of the heart, is the place where resides our Spirit, our true Self, which is eternally pure and unaffected by anything, like a shining diamond hidden within us which witnesses all our actions.

After Self Realisation, our attention becomes for the first time connected to our Spirit and we gradually become aware of it. Our misidentifications with our ego or conditionings drop and we start becoming identified with our Spirit, which is our true nature.

On the physical level, this chakra looks after our heart and lungs—if affected it can cause asthma or various heart conditions.

It is from our heart that the compassion and love manifests, and also the heart chakra is the one that gives us the sense of responsibility and pure behaviour towards others. The heart chakra manifests in the center (at the level of the sternum bone) as complete security and confidence. All our worries, doubts and fears are destroyed when the heart chakra is fully enlightened by the Kundalini.

7.5. VISHUDDHI CHAKRA

The fifth chakra is the chakra of diplomacy, of pure relationships with others, and of playful detachment. It removes all our guilts and remorses when it is opened by the Kundalini, and gives us a kind and compassionate voice. The tendencies to dominate others or to feel dominated by others, the feelings of superiority or inferiority and all jealousies are removed when this chakra is nourished by the Kundalini.

Also, the Vishuddhi is the chakra which gives us the connection with the whole, enabling us to feel our oneness and the fact that we are all part and parcel of the whole.

7.6. THE AGNYA CHAKRA

The sixth chakra is the chakra of forgiveness and compassion. Forgiveness is the power to let go of anger, hatred and resentment and to discover, in humility, the nobility and generosity of the Spirit.

It is the one that dissolves all our ego, conditionings, habits, false ideas of racialism, and all our misidentifications. It is the narrow gate which opens the way for our consciousness to ascend to its final destination, which is the seventh center.

Roving eyes, watching impure things, or self-centeredness damage this chakra. Watching the sky, earth or nature can help cleanse it.

7.7. THE SAHASRARA CHAKRA

The seventh center integrates all the chakras with their respective qualities. It is the last milestone of the evolution of human awareness.

Nowadays, we are at a level which corresponds to this chakra, and our consciousness is able to easily enter into this new realm of perception, which is beyond our limited mind and concepts, and which becomes absolute at the level of the Sahasrara. This chakra gives us the direct, absolute perception of Reality on our central nervous system.

This is precisely what is achieved by Self Realisation, through the spontaneous awakening of the Kundalini given by Sahaja Yoga.

7.8. ACTIVATE OUR CHAKRAS

There are certain ways that we consciously can activate our chakras: through the breath, through yoga postures, meditation and prayers, through sound and colour, and through our singing voice, which is intimately connected to the chakras, through the powerful combination of thinking and feeling in visualisation, and through certain kind of music.

While the soul is still in an undeveloped, unconscious state our freedom of choice is very limited. We can choose if we want our coffee with or without sugar, if we like this thing or that one. But as far as our destiny goes, we are like leaves on the ground, blown by the wind, victims of circumstances. We obey blindly the laws of the tribe and are concerned primarily with our physical survival.

Only when we wake up to the truth that we are spiritual beings, incarnating for a short while into a physical world and having physical experiences for the growth and learning of our souls, only then do we get some freedom of choice. At that stage it is of utmost importance to realise that our freedom of choice is about our allegiances: are we making the choices from a spiritual point of view, that will bring light, goodness, love and peace into the world, or do we choose to identify wholly with materialism and egoism, giving in to lust for power, control, judgement, hatred and divisive manipulations? This is the chakra where we discover our allegiances.

We can honour our oneness with all and serve all, each other and the world we live in, with respect, justice and compassion, or we can give in to tribal group consciousness. We can withdraw from each other, fear and hate what we do not know or understand, try to impose our will and our views on others without respecting their individuality, and continue to divide and fragment the world. But where will that take us in the long run - or short run?

Let us choose oneness in love and readiness to share, in respect for creation in all its magnificent manifestations throughout the mineral, plant, animal and human kingdoms. Let us serve each other, not destroy each other.

We come into this world with just two main tasks:

1) to learn and

2) to teach

We all have our individual lessons to learn for our soul's growth and progress. As we learn these lessons, the entire planet learns them through us and greater balance is attained in the universe. Because remember, we are part of "All"—humanity, this planet, the whole of creation—and we have to learn that "All is One".

We all come here to be each other's teachers. Before we incarnated we made a contract and planned what we would work on and learn during this life-time. We promised to share with others our knowledge and wisdom and the energy that the universe has invested in us. Our only choice, once we enter the earth plane, is whether we share our gifts in a positive or negative way. We can share willingly and lovingly, or in such negative ways that others learn from us what not do.

If we choose the positive way, we will move faster and more effortlessly through all obstacles and difficulties. If we choose the negative way our life will deteriorate more and more into complete confusion and greater suffering.

8

KUNDALINI ENERGY

Kundalini is a dormant energy within most peple. In Hindu mythology, Kundalini is a serpent goddess who lies asleep at the base of the spine, coiled three and a half times around the first chakra. Her name is Kundalini Shakti, and she represents the unfolding of the divine Shakti energy, the energizing potential of life itself, a living goddess who enlivens all things.

Under certain circumstances, the Kundalini energy awakens and begins to rise through the body, piercing and opening the chakras as she moves in her undulating, snake-like fashion. As Kundalini releases stored and blocked energies, her movement can be quite intense, sometimes painful, and often leads to mental states that seem out of this world.

Circumstances that stimulate Kundalini awakening are many and varied, but are usually triggered by such things as extended periods of meditation, yoga, fasting, stress, trauma, psychedelic drugs, or near death experiences. Kundalini is a condensed, primal force, similar to the potential energy found in water. When released, it creates a vertical connection between the chakras by opening the subtle channels known as nadi, most specifically, the central channel that moves up the spine called sushumna. If we put water through a small hose at very high pressure, the end of the hose will undulate like a snake. Similarly, the intense energy of Kundalini undulates in the body as it rises through the chakras.

Kundalini can also be seen as a result of the chakras connecting to each other. Theoretically, as the chakras enlarge, the spinning of one can enchance the spinning of the one above or below it. Kundalini is basically a healing force, but its effects can sometimes be quite unpleasant. Such effects may last for minutes, days, months, or even years.

If you find yourself dealing with uncomfortable Kundalini awakening symptoms, you should:

1. Purify the body. Abstain from recreational drugs, tobacco, alcohol, and caffein, prescription drugs. Avoid food additives, high sugars, or greasy foods. Eat well, especially protein which is generally grounding. Get massage and vigorous exercise.
2. Reduce stress. If you are in for a major spiritual transformation, make time for the necessary changes in your life. You may need to devote more time to your spirituality or health.
3. Find Support. Find other who have knowledge of this experience.
4. Educate yourself.
5. Treat underlying psychological issues. As Kundalini brings up unresolved issues, this is the best time to deal with them. It will make the ride smoother.
6. Examine your spiritual practices. If you have not been practicing meditation, yoga or some spiritual practice, it may be time to begin. You might need to stop meditating for a while if it increases unpleasant Kundalini awakening symptoms.

7. Practice grounding. Kundalini is most difficult when the energy is moving upward without enough energy moving downward to balance. Investigate the possibility of the first chakra issues that need to be resolved in order to give a firmer base. Practice grounding exercise daily.

8.1. STAGES IN KUNDALINI AWAKENING

There are seven major chakras, the left and right energies of Ida and Pingala, and the Sushumna nadi, the central channel that courses through the chakras (Sushumna is sometimes called "silver cord"). Following are the stages of kundalini awakening

— Prana usually flow in Ida *or* Pingala

— Prana is made to flow in Ida *and* Pingala

— Prana is made to flow in Sushumna

— Kundalini energy is awakened

— Kundalini is lead upwards

— Kundalini rises to Sahasrara

8.1.1. Prana Usually flows in Ida *or* Pingala

Our energy system is usually more active in either the left or right sides, which are the Ida and Pingala. Of the thousands of energy channels (nadis), three are most important: Ida, Pingala, and Sushumna (sometimes called "silver cord"), which is the central channel, and the most important.

Solar and lunar breaths: The breath and the underlying energy, or Prana, usually flow predominantly on one side or other, the left or the right. Breath predominantly in the left nostril is described as cool, and sometimes referred to as feminine. The flow of Prana on the left is the lunar, and is called *Ida*. Breath flowing predominantly in the right nostril is described as hot, and sometimes referred to as masculine. The flow of Prana on the right is the solar, and is called *Pingala*.

Nostril dominance shifts: Usually we believe that we are breathing through both nostrils, although breath is normally dominant in one or the other. The dominance shifts from time to time during the day. For one with a well balanced body and mind, that shift of nostril dominance happens approximately once in ninety minutes. For other people, the shift may be much different. Sometimes one can be so off balance that one nostril remains dominant, which is a symptom of some physical, mental, or emotional difficulties.

Prana is the first energy: The word Prana comes from two roots. *Pra* means first, and *na* is the smallest unit of energy. Prana is therefore the first breath, the primal or atomic beginning of the flow of energy. Out of this first unit of energy manifests all aspects and levels of the human being.

Prana flows in nadis: That Prana flows in certain patterns, or lines, or channels that are called *nadis*. There are said to be some 72,000 such nadis coursing through the subtle body that supports the physical body and its various systems. When the Prana flows across the latent impressions, they spring to life in the form of awareness in the conscious mind, in the physical body and brain.

Intersections of the nadis are chakras: Those thousands of nadis intersect here and there, forming the matrix of the subtle body. The major intersections are called chakras, and the five elements of earth, water, fire, air, and space manifest around these so as to form the gross body. Often, we speak of chakras as if they are *in* the body. Actually, this is somewhat backwards. It is more like the body has been suspended *on* the subtle chakras, with these chakras being formed or constructed by the major highway intersections of the nadis.

Caduceus of medicine: The caduceus is the symbol of medicine. The root meaning of medicine or medicate means attention, which is also the root of meditation. Thus, we have attending physicians, and we pay attention in meditation. The caduceus is a winged staff, with two serpents, and is carried by the Greek god, Hermes, who is said to be the messenger of the Gods. Together, Ida and Pingala form the snakes of the caduceus, while Sushumna forms the staff. The snakes intersect at the chakras, as do the nadis described above. At the ajna chakra, between the eyebrows, there are two petals, one on either side, just as there are two wings at the top of the caduceus.

Prana divides itself into five Vayus: When the Prana operates in the body, it divides into five major flows called Vayus. These can be thought of as somewhat like major currents in one of the large oceans of the world, while there may be thousands of smaller currents. These five Vayus are the major currents that contain thousands of smaller currents.

1. Prana Vayu operates from the heart area, and is an upward flowing energy, having to do with vitalizing life forces.
2. Apana Vayu operates from the base of the torso, in the rectum area, is a downward flowing energy, and has to do with eliminating or throwing off what is no longer needed.
3. Samana Vayu operates from the navel area, deals with digestion, and allows the mental discrimination between useful and not useful thoughts.
4. Udana Vayu operates from the throat and drives exhalation, operating in conjunction with Prana Vayu, which deals with inhalation.

5. Vyana Vayu operates throughout the whole body, having no particular center, and is a coordinating energy throughout the various systems.

Prana drives the ten indriyas: Prana is the source of energy that operates the ten indriyas. Five are the karmendriyas or instruments of actions, which are elimination, procreation, motion, grasping and speaking. Five are the jnanendriyas or cognitive senses, which are smelling, tasting, seeing, touching, and hearing. These ten operate through the chakras, and receive their power from the Prana.

8.1.2. Prana is Made to Flow in Ida *and* Pingala

The first step in Kundalini Awakening is balancing the flow of energy in Ida and Pingala. This means that equal amounts of Prana are flowing in the left and right sides. It is most readily evidenced by the breath flowing evenly in the two nostrils.

In our common language, we speak of feeling *off-balance* or getting *balanced*. To *balance* or *center* the energies is the goal of this step of the Kundalini Awakening process. This affects not only the subtle body, but is also experienced in the gross, physical body, and brings tremendous health benefits by positively regulating the autonomic nervous system.

Transitions between Ida and Pingala: There is a natural transition between Ida and Pingala from time to time during the day. For those with very healthy bodies and minds, this shift happens approximately every 90 minutes. For others, the shift may not follow so naturally, or energy may be more or less stuck in either Ida or Pingala for much longer periods of time during the 24 hours of the day.

Transitions bring calmness to the mind: In these moments of natural transition, the mind is calm, centered, or balanced. There is a sense of inner peace, as if the mind wants to do nothing but be in meditation. For most of us, unaware of this transition, we force ourselves to stay with the matters at hand in the external world during these moments, possibly thinking we are just sleepy. Once you are aware of this natural shifting, it can provide a time to take just a minute for yourself to enjoy the inner stillness. It is as if nature is giving us a *free* meditation from time to time.

Sandhya, the wedding: The union or balancing of Ida and Pingala is like a marriage. It is the wedding of sun and moon, night and day. This wedding is called *sandhya*, and like with a marriage, is a time of great joy, only this is a meditative joy. In this wedding even the mind and the breath are joined in a happy union.

Beginning of joy in meditation: This balancing of Ida and Pingala, and causing Prana to flow evenly, this wedding of sun and moon, is the real beginning of joy in meditation. All of the other practices up to this stage are to bring this state of peaceful mind, from where the real practice of meditation begins. From this point, meditation is a joy, not a discipline. For, why would anybody have to cultivate discipline to do that which is only bringing joy?

Even breath between the nostrils: At one's regularly scheduled time for Yoga meditation, the aspirant wants to be able to balance these two energies by direct control. Breath balancing practices are done so as to balance Ida and Pingala, allowing them to flow evenly. These practices are extremely useful and build a foundation for Kundalini Awakening.

Opening a nostril with the mind: The ability to regulate this balance of breath by focusing the mind on the flow in the nostrils, though a simple practice, is one of the most profound parts of the inner journey. Notice with your mind which nostril is flowing more, and which is flowing less freely. By focusing attention on the closed or less open nostril, it will gradually open, and bring an increased feeling of calm. This may take some months to accomplish, or it may come sooner, but the skill will definitely come with practice.

Alternate nostril breathing: Alternate nostril breathing is a specific practice to balance Ida and Pingala, whereby you intentionally breathe through one, and then the other nostril. It may be done either with the fingers or the intentionality of the mind. There are many combinations of alternate nostril breathing, though one of the simplest is to breath three exhalations and inhalations from one nostril, and then three from the other. This is called one *round* of alternate nostril breathing. Three rounds is generally done to complete the practice.

Soham mantra: The breath naturally makes two sounds, *Sooooooo* with inhalation, and *Hummmmmm* with exhalation. Conscious use of the soham mantra is a tremendous aid in balancing Ida and Pingala.

Hatha Yoga balances Ida and Pingala: The entire purpose of Hatha Yoga is the balancing of these energies of Ida and Pingala. *Ha* means *sun* and *tha* means *moon*. The sun is the active energy of Pingala, whereas moon is the passive energy of Ida. The union of these two energies is called Yoga, which means union or wholeness.

The Hatha postures and breathing practices all help lead one to balance between Ida and Pingala, where they are both flowing freely. The breathing practices of Diaphragmatic Breathing and Two-to-One Breathing are especially helpful, and the vigorous breathing practices such as Kapalabhati and Bhastrika can help to break the pattern of being stuck in Ida or Pingala.

Autonomic nervous system: Balancing Ida and Pingala also balances the sympathetic and parasympathetic branches of the autonomic nervous system, reducing the elevated flight or fight response. In other words, the single act of balancing the breath is a tremendous aid in physical stress reduction, in addition to being a spiritual practice setting the stage for Kundalini Awakening.

8.1.3. Prana to Flow in Sushumna

When the Prana is not only balanced, left and right, but is also made to flow through the central channel of Sushumna (sometimes called "silver cord"), there comes an even deeper, abiding peace of mind. The mind and heart only want to go inside for meditation.

The two energies of Ida and Pingala flow along the spine (meru danda) of the subtle body. Ida flows along the left side, and Pingala flows along the right. Sushumna nadi flows directly upwards and downwards, between Ida and Pingala, coursing through the chakras. Within the many ganglionated cords of the nervous system, there is a nerve center in the area of the ajna chakra, at the space between the eyebrows, that is called the ganglion of ribes. Although Ida and Pingala are subtle energy flows, they correspond to this physical structure. Ida flows along the left side of the spine, circles the ganglion of ribes, and converges on its left side. Pingala flows along the right side of the spine, circles the ganglion of ribes, and converges on its right side. Thus, the two forces of Ida and Pingala converge at the ganglion of ribes, in the space between the eyebrows, the ajna chakra.

Meditation at ajna chakra: Because of this convergence of Ida and Pingala at the point of the ganglion of ribes and the ajna chakra, meditation on this space is extremely useful and often recommended. For those who have the ability to gently focus here, there is great benefit in calming the gross breath, balancing Ida and Pingala, and stilling the mind. It is because of this, in part, that the Bhagavad Gita recommends gently keeping out all external contacts, and internally placing attention between the eyebrows, making the energies flow evenly between the nostrils.

Breath at the nostrils: One of the most direct means of balancing the energies and causing prana to flow in Sushumna is by attention of mind on the flow of breath at the nostrils. By attending to the lesser flowing nostril, it will gradually open. By attending to the other, they will both flow more freely. When attending to both as one steady flow, the peace of Sushumna awakening gradually comes. While this practice can sound very simple, it requires a gentle persistence and a good ability to focus attention.

Yoga Nidra: Bringing prana into Sushumna balances the chakras and prepares the pathway for Kundalini once it awakens and begins to rise. Bhuta Shuddhi is also quite useful in balancing the energy and allowing it to flow in sushumna.

Ida and Pingala also join at the ganglion impar: The ganglion impar is the lower termination point of the sympathetic nervous system. It is anterior to the sacrococcygeal junction, or in front of the coccyx, corresponding to the location of the muladhara chakra. The two flows of Ida and Pingala also join at this lower end of the subtle anatomy.

Between the ganglion of ribes and the ganglion impar: Ida and Pingala flow between these two points and are in constant contact with the nervous system and the central channel of the subtle spine. While one may meditate on the ajna chakra, the upper joining point noted above, there is also great utility in meditation practices that move up and down along this central channel between these two points. This can have a tremendous effect on balancing the energies, calming the mind, and allowing the Prana to flow through the central channel of Sushumna.

Root lock and Prana: The root lock, or mulabandha is performed by contracting the perineum muscles that are in the flat space between the genital area the anus. By contracting this muscle group, the normally downward flowing energy (Apana Vayu) is pulled upwards, gradually uniting with the normally upward flowing energy (Prana Vayu) at the navel center. The root lock has the effect of causing Prana to flow in Sushumna channel, rather than along Ida and Pingala. Eventually, the practice is combined with other practices, so as to cause Kundalini to awaken and arise.

Prana enters the mouth of Sushumna: At the first chakra (muladhara) is the root (kanda) out of which all of the subtle energy channels (nadis) originate and go outward throughout the subtle body. It is located at the perineum, between the genitals and the anus. At this root is the mouth or opening to the Sushumna channel, as well as chitrini nadi and other finer nadis that are within the Sushumna, like a fine stream inside of a fine hose. After Ida and Pingala are balanced, the Prana is guided to enter and flow into the mouth of Sushumna.

Sushumna Awakening is sustained: Rather than being a temporary experience that happens during the natural transition of breath dominance, the balanced flow of Prana is now sustained for a longer time during the period of meditation. Also, the Prana is now flowing more in the Sushumna channel itself, rather than just being balanced between left and right. Sometimes this flow of Prana is experienced as a feeling sensation in the spine, possibly as a warmth of energy flow.

Note that while this is a very important stage, and skill to acquire, this is *not* full Kundalini Awakening, but is the flow of the Prana through the central channel. This flow of Prana in Sushumna is sometimes thought by people to be Kundalini Awakening, which it is not. Recall the metaphor of Prana being like the steam arising from the bowl of hot water, and reflect on the difference between the steam and the significantly more concentrated water in the pot.

This flow of Prana in Sushumna is one of the first goals of meditation. Of the eight rungs of Yoga, numbers three and four work with your sitting posture and breathing or pranayama. When the breath is balanced, and the Prana is flowing in Sushumna, the senses truly begin to turn inward, which is Pratyahara, the fifth of the eight rungs. It sets the stage for deeper meditation and samadhi.

When the Prana flows through Sushumna, the body seems indestructible, as it has been left behind in attention. One begins to experience fearlessness, or so it seems. It is a surface level of fearlessness, related to mind and the possible events of the world. Still deeper is the fear related to loss of individuality itself. So this fearlessness, however nice it is, is still not the fearlessness that comes from being one with the One.

Prana flowing in Sushumna is extremely peaceful, and can easily be confused with Kundalini Awakening. As you feel the tranquility, along with the warmth flowing through the levels of the spine, this calmness is very alluring, and when reading the books about Kundalini Awakening, it can seem as if, "This is it!" There is a difference between the flow of Prana through Sushumna and full Kundalini Awakening, with that Kundalini energy itself rising. Both Prana and Kundalini are forms of the universal energy of Shakti, though here, at this stage, it is still Prana that is flowing in Sushumna.

8.1.4. Awakening the Kundalini Energy

Kundalini Awakening may ultimately occur with all methods, even those that do not seem to be directly related to Kundalini. Thus, we have two general approaches with the various practices, those that are more *immediate* and those that are more *mediate*. The specific practices may overlap, or be part of both approaches.

1. *Immediate methods*: *Immediate* means direct; not acting through a secondary agency, method, or practice; the quicker, more forceful approach. The *immediate* or direct approach might involve the various asanas, locks, and breathing practices, as well as more intense meditation practices. It may include Hatha Yoga, Kriya Yoga, Kundalini Yoga, Raja Yoga, and Tantra Yoga. With these approaches, it is important to have external guidance so as to learn properly.
2. *Mediate methods*: *Mediate* means indirect; acting through a secondary agency, method, or practices; the slower, more gentle approach. The *mediate* or indirect approach might involve religious rituals, Bhakti Yoga (devotional), Jnana Yoga (self-enquiry), Karma Yoga (action in the world), simple mantra chanting, gentler meditation focusing on more gross level objects. These approaches are more suited to practice without guidance, though it is beneficial and recommended.
3. *Methods of awakening Kundalini*: For the intentional, immediate or direct awakening of Kundalini, there are several categories of practices, and these are generally chosen in alignment with one's particular teacher and tradition:

   — *Physical*: These methods involve Hatha Yoga postures, Mudras (gestures), and Bandhas (locks).

— *Breath*: Vigorous breathing practices (Pranayama), along with the Bandhas, and breath retention.

— *Meditation*: The intensity of concentration leading to Meditation and various levels of Samadhi.

— *Mantra*: Some of the Mantra schools work with subtle vibrations to awaken the various aspects of latent energy.

Along the way, some of the obstacles may be removed, as well as glimpses of Kundalini Awakening be given through Shaktipata, the gift of consciousness called grace (kripa) or guru, whereby a transference of energy happens, somewhat like a magnet affects some metal objects. It may come in a single, large burst, though more often it comes in smaller experiences along the way.

There are various signs and symptoms of Kundalini Awakening, and these may be of varying duration and intensity. Some of the experiences may seem similar to those of Prana flowing in Sushumna, though the intensity is quite different. The specific experiences may also vary from person to person, and the words used to describe the experiences may be different. The nature of the experience is also affected by the degree to which the individual chakras are involved in the energy increase. However, there are some general signs and symptoms that are commonly reported:

1. Involuntary jerkiness or shaking in the body,
2. Intense feelings of pleasure or bliss,
3. Feelings of cold in the body,
4. Intense heat in the spine, or a particular chakra, as if molten metal were flowing in the spine,
5. Striking flows of energy, like electricity or internal lightning bolts,

6. Feelings like snakes or ants crawling on the body, particularly along the spine, or between the feet and head,
7. Mudras (hand gestures), Bandhas (locks), Asanas (postures), or Pranayama (breathing practices) may come spontaneously rather than being intentionally practiced,
8. A sense of confusion or uncertainty about what is happening in these experiences,
9. Spontaneous emotional shifts or mood swings,
10. Increase in the experience of inner colors and lights,
11. Inner sounds, such as musical instruments, buzzing, roaring, or thunder,
12. Waves of creative, intellectual, or spiritual insights.

8.1.5. Kundalini Rises to Sahasrara

Once the Kundalini Shakti attains the state of union with the pure consciousness at the sahasrara, there is no longer any unconscious during that time. There is no longer a latent aspect, as full illumination has come, eliminating this polarization of active and latent. Awareness of the body and the external world is withdrawn into the highest samadhi.

Body is in mind; mind is not in body: One comes to see in experience the truth that all of the body is in the mind, but that not all of the mind is in the body, as it usually seems. To the external view of other people, the body of one in this heightened state of union may appear to be dead. It may be cold to the touch, and there may be no perceptible vital signs, such as a pulse. The body continues to function so that it might be used again after the individuality returns.

Involution and evolution: The process towards realizing and abiding in pure consciousness is one of evolution. The involution of consciousness into the human being is conceptualized as being a process of the creative energy of Shakti condensing further and further into solid form, and falling asleep at the first chakra, at the perineum near the base of the spine. The process of Kundalini Awakening reverses this involution until the full potential of the human is realized in the return to the pure consciousness.

Sat chit ananda: The realization of the true Self is best described as indescribable. However, for convenience sake it is sometimes described as being the nature of sat, chit, and ananda. Sat means existence itself. Chit means consciousness. Ananda means bliss.

8.2. KUNDALINI REIKI

Kundalini Reiki can also help with problems with this energy. It will safely and gently awaken it. If awakened Kundalini will complete the cleansing and purification of body layers, chakras and energy channels. With additional Reiki energy this process will become faster and smoother. When the body layers are cleansed it will increase our energy vibration and expand our consciousness. By opening the Kundalini the personal development process will accelerate.

The entrance for the Kundalini energy is through the First or Base chakra which connects us to the Earth energy. It runs through the main energy channel and out of the Crown chakra. The two most basic forms of energy reach the human system from the base and the krown chakra. These two chakras are linked by the Sushumna, which is connected to the rest of the chakras by their "stems".

These stems provide the chakras with essential energy. The Sushumna is at the same time the channel through which the Kundalini energy is stimulated. When it is stimulated, its energy is converted into various frequences for each of the chakras. The energy is manifested via the lowest frequences of the base chakra, and highest frequences of the crown chakra.

These converted frequences are conveyed to the subtle bodies and to physical body, and they are percived by us as sensations, emotions, and thoughts.

There are also three levels of attunements in Kundalini Reiki and it must begin with level 1.

8.2.1. Level 1

This attunement is the equivalent to Usui Reiki 1-2-3 attunements. It opens the healing channels to allow channelling of Reiki energy. The Crown, Heart and Hand chakras are opened and strengthened. At the same time you are prepared for the Kundalini awakening in the 2nd attunement. You are also taught to perform a complete healing treatment and to heal remotely.

8.2.2. Level 2

The Reiki channels are strengthened. Kundalini energy reaches minimum the Solar Plexus Chakra preparing for the full Kundalini awakening in Reiki 3. You learn a specific meditation which increases the Kundalini energy. A chakra and energy system cleansing takes place.

8.2.3. Level 3

The Troat, Solar Plexus, Hara and Root Chakras are opened. A full rising of the Kundalini energy takes place. You learn to pass on Kundalini Reiki 1-2-3.

Regular practice of Yoga and/or meditation will help the Kundalini energy awakening, but usually it takes years of practice.

Kundalini energy awakening and raising has never been easier. You can now save years of meditation by using this New and Exciting Harmonic System of Tantra Yoga. Each chakra has an associated colour and vibration. Each chakra vibration has been synthesized in the laboratory and recorded. If you listen to the specific chakra vibration—that chakra is stimulated. If you listen to the chakra vibrations in the correct sequence it simulates the process of "raising the Kundalini".

9

HOW TO AWAKEN THE SPIRIT

9.1. BEGINNING OF SPIRITUAL EMERGENCE

No one knows for certain just what kick starts the unfolding of spiritual potential. For some, spiritual emergence is a gentle and integrated process which develops as a natural consequence of many years dedicated to service and prayer or meditation under the guidance of a teacher or guru. Others may experience a more abrupt awakening, possible due to practices which awaken transformative energy before the person has done the necessary groundwork.

It is thought that practices such as yoga, bioenergetics, polarity work or breathwork cause the awakening of Kundalini energy which heralds the transformation of spiritual potential. Kundalini is the Hindu word for the sacred, transformative energy that awakens consciousness. According to esoteric literature, this energy has been coiled at the base of the spine in a latent form since birth, awaiting the stimulus to unfold its potential.

As this energy becomes active, it is usually sensed as a vibrational or energetic force in the body, together with a strong sense of spirit. Its movement may be experienced as a rushing, outpouring, a steady streaming up the spine, or a slowly coiling spiral motion. Another common catalyst seems to be intense physical or emotional distress.

As people confront the limits of their endurance and come face to face with death, they will often move into non ordinary or transpersonal states of consciousness. Thus experiences with natural disasters, near death experiences, or life transitions such as pregnancy, midlife or separation, may be emotionally tense situations which can lead to spiritual awakening. Regardless of the specifics of each individual's experience, the Kundalini awakening heralds a great period of change in a person's life.

When spiritual seekers or even those who do not consider themselves to be on a spiritual path find themselves experiencing levels of awareness or energy transformation that they are unable to handle or for which they have no reference, then the result can be a state of emergency. In this state, a person feels highly vulnerable and oversensitive to incoming stimuli. Typically they feel overwhelmed, fragmented, fearful, confused and disoriented. With their absorption in inner processes, they may not be able to look after even basic self care.

All these situations can be bewildering and frightening, and at these times these people need support and reassurance as they undergo their transformations. The spiritual emergency network in the US seeks to network people and provide information to facilitate a more gentle emergence of spiritual potentials. The network is intended to put people in touch with others who have undergone similar experiences, or with counsellors who are aware of spiritual dimensions of reality.

9.2. KUNDALINI AWAKENING SYMPTOMS

While the awakening Kundalini may be a dramatic experience, the resultant shift in consciousness may be accompanied by years of physical and psychological upheavals. The process of Kundalini awakening can vary greatly from person to person. Some have intense physical symptoms, while others experience mainly emotional or psychological symptoms. It is as if the new energy invites a spring cleaning throughout the entire system, with unresolved physical or emotional conditions coming up for resolution and release.

The life transforming changes which accompany a Kundalini awakening cover the entire physiological, emotional, mental and spiritual spectrum. There are seven categories of symptoms which have been observed during Kundalini awakening .

9.2.1. Pranic Movements or Kriyas

Prana is the Hindu word for vital energy. Thus as intense energy moves through the body and clears out physiological blocks, a person may experience intense involuntary, jerking movements of the body, including shaking, vibrations, spasm and contraction. As deeply held armouring and blockages to the smooth flow of energy are released, the person may re-access memories and emotions associated with past trauma and injury.

9.2.2. Yogic Phenomena

Some people find themselves performing yogic postures or hand mudra gestures which they have never learned or could not do in a normal state of consciousness. Similarly, they may produce Sanskrit words or sounds, or have an awareness of inner music or sound, mantras or tones. Unusual breathing patterns may appear with either very rapid or slow, shallow breathing. Some people may not breathe at all for extended periods.

9.2.3. Physiological Symptoms

A Kundalini awakening often generates unusual physiological activity as intense movement of energy releases toxins in the body. Symptoms include apparent heart problems, pains in head and spine, gastrointestinal disturbances and nervous problems. Internal sensations have been reported as sensations of burning, oversensitivity to sensory input, hyperactivity or lethargy, great variations in sexual desire and even spontaneous orgasm. Symptoms can be erratic, coming and going without provocation, but are generally unresponsive to medical treatment.

9.2.4. Psychological Upheaval

Spiritual awakening offers a direct challenge to the primacy of ego consciousness and the myth of separation. It brings with it a challenge to move beyond the unconscious responses ruled by drives and instincts and remove ego consciousness from the centre stage of the psyche. It comes as no surprise that such a challenge produces a period of confusion and unbalance.

People find themselves beset by inexplicable emotional states as they move to clear out unresolved issues. The emotional roller coaster may swing from feelings of anxiety, guilt and depression, through to compassion, love and joy, with accompanying bouts of uncontrollable weeping.

9.2.5. Extra Sensory Experiences

As perception expands outside of consensus reality, people experience atypical visual phenomena, including visions of lights, symbols, entities, or review of past life experiences. Auditory input may include hearing voices, music, inner sounds or mantras. Even the olfactory system may be stimulated with perception of scents of sandalwood, rose or incense. There may also be disruption of the proprioceptive system, with losing a sense of self as a body, or feeling bigger than the body, or out of the body, with the resulting confusion and disorientation.

9.2.6. Psychic Phenomena

With the opening up of psychic abilities, a person may experience precognition, telepathy, psychokinesis, awareness of auras and healing abilities.

9.2.7. Mystical States of Consciousness

A person may shift into altered states of consciousness where they directly perceive the unity underlying the world of separation and experience a deep peace and serenity with a profound knowing of wisdom.

In some cases, the state of emergency due to psychological upheaval is so acute that it resembles a psychotic episode. Many clinicians still regard phenomena associated with spiritual emergence as indicative of pathology because the signs are so easily confused with the indicators of psychosis, mania, depression, schizophrenia or borderline personality disorder. Many people undergoing spiritual emergency are misdiagnosed and treated with suppressive medication which further complicates their process.

When Kundalini awakening happens to people who are not on a spiritual path or who have no context or framework to understand the bewildering upheaval of mind, body and spirit, the experience can leave them fragile and fragmented. As the Kundalini process involves a redefinition and reintegration of self, it adds extra pressure when health professionals or significant others wish to suppress the transformation and insist that the person conforms to old ways of being in the world.

Of greatest benefit is a supportive framework which can allow people to make sense of the intricate connection between spirit and the movement of physical energy in the body, rather than fearing they are going insane. It is more empowering to understand that Kundalini awakening is a process which taps into the blueprint for higher consciousness which is latent within every human. While the enormous changes associated with a spiritual awakening may demand psychological and social adjustments, they are not in themselves necessarily indicative of illness.

Communication and connection with others who can provide support and a meaningful context for understanding the process reduces the isolation and overwhelm and can help to minimise the disturbance. Someone who has the personal qualities of creative adaptation to change and a flexible mental framework is more likely to weather the changes with grace and style than someone who is rigid in their beliefs and world view.

9.3. KUNDALINI AWAKENING WITH ENLIGHTENMENT

It is important not to confuse Kundalini awakening with enlightenment. Enlightenment rarely results from a single encounter with the numinous. It is more as if the energetic awakening initiates an expansion in consciousness which sets the scene for a progression of many experiences with transpersonal states of consciousness. The intensity and duration of each of glimpse varies with our readiness to contain and integrate them.

Thus the Kundalini awakening is not an end point in itself, but the beginning of a transformation of consciousness which expands our capacity to KNOW the infinite. Spiritual emergence often includes expanded perceptual abilities, increased energy, creative expression and a dedication to being of service for the greater good.

10

KUNDALINI: AWAKENING THE SERPENT POWER

In yogic terms, our thoughts and actions for the most part follow the path of least resistance. That is to say, they are overdetermined by the energetic template of the subtle body. This explains why it is so difficult to change our behaviour even when we have realized that our old patterns are wrong, unproductive, or damaging. Hence, in addition to behavioural change, the Tantric practitioners attempt to modify the pathways of the life force directly. This modification is a matter of cleansing the nadis-a practice called nadi shodhana

The kundalini in itself is neither good nor bad. It simply is the Goddess energy as it manifests in the human body. Unless we consciously collaborate with it, it remains on the most subtle level of existence, sustaining us through the agency of the life force (prana) but never entering our field of awareness. Through self-purification and an appropriate course of disciplines, we can benefit from it more immediately by inviting it into our life as a powerful transformative force.

In its hidden state, the kundalini is said to be sheer potentiality. This is only relatively correct, for the Goddess energy is always active on our behalf, maintaining all the subtle energetic processes that underlie our physical and mental structures and functions. In its awakened state, however, the kundalini is an incredible agency of transformation, spiritual growth, and at last enlightenment.

Various postures (asana) are said to effect the purification of the conduits or channels (nadi). The Hatha-Yoga-Prad-pika singles out the adept's posture (siddha-asana) as being particularly suited for this purpose, but other scriptures favour different postures. The adept's posture is practiced by placing the left heel at the rectum and the right heel above the genitals, while resting the chin on the chest and gazing at the spot between the eyebrows. Sometimes the position of the legs is reversed. The potency of this very popular posture derives from the fact that it balances the subtle energies and thereby awakens the serpent power.

While postures like the siddha-asana are important, the principal means of cleansing the channels is controlled breathing, as it has been elaborated in great detail in the scriptures of Hatha-Yoga. The Gheranda-Samhita distinguishes between two basic types of purification practices: samanu and nirmanu, which terms denote "mental" and "nonmental" respectively. In physical cleansing processes called dhauti, comprising the following techniques:

1. antar-dhauti ("inner cleansing") consisting of the following four techniques:
   a) vata-sara ("air process"), which is done by inhaling through the mouth and expelling the air through the lower passage;
   b) vari-sara ("water process"), which is done by sipping water until the stomach is completely filled and expelling it through the lower passage;

   c) vahni-sara ("fire process"), which is done by pushing the navel one hundred times back toward the spine, which increased the "gastric fire";

   d) bahish-krita ("external action"), which is done by sucking in air through the mouth until the stomach is filled, retaining it for ninety minutes, and then expelling it through the lower passage; this is followed by one's standing in navel-deep water and pushing out the lower intestinal tract for cleansing;

2. danta-dhauti ("dental cleansing"), which includes cleaning the teeth, the tongue, as well as the ears and frontal sinuses;
3. hrid-dhauti ("lit". "heart cleansing"), which consists of (a) introducing the stalk of a plantain, turmeric, or cane into the throat to clean it out; (b) filling the stomach with water and then expelling it through the mouth; (c) swallowing a long strip of thin cloth and then pulling it out again (a process called vâso-dhauti, "cloth cleansing");
4. mula-shodhana ("rectal cleansing"), which is done by means of turmeric, water, or the middle finger;

In our body we have five elements. The element responsible for production of the elixir of life (prana) is earth. The element of air is used as a churning rod, through inhalation and exhalation, and distribution is through the element of ether. Ether is space, and its quality is that it can contract or expand. When you inhale, the element of ether expands to take the breath in. In exhalation, the ether contracts to push out toxins.

Two elements remain: water and fire. If there is a fire, water is used to extinguish it. This gives us the idea that fire and water are opposing elements. With the help of the elements of earth, air and ether, a friction is created between water and fire, which not only generates energy but releases it, just as water moving turbines in a hydroelectric power station produces electricity. To generate electricity, the water has to flow at a certain speed. An inadequate flow will not produce electricity. Similarly, in our system, normal breathing does not produce that intense energy. This is why we are all suffering fro stress and strain, causing poor circulation which affects our health and happiness. The current is not sufficient so we are merely existing, not living.

In the practice of pranayama, we make the breath very long. In this way, the elements of fire and water are brought together, and this contact of fire and water in the body, with the help of the element of air, releases a new energy, called by yogis divine energy, or kundalini shakti, and this is the energy of prana.

Other texts recommend similar procedures in which the left and the right pathway of the life force are alternately activated. According to the Shiva-Samhita, alternate breathing should be performed twenty times four times a day-at dawn, mid-day, sunset, and mid-night. If done regularly for three months, this procedure, we are told, will definitely cleanse the channels. It is only then that the practitioner should turn to breath control proper.

The Shiva-Samhitâ also states that when the nadis have been purified, certain signs will manifest: The body becomes harmonious (sama) and beautiful, and emits a pleasant scent, while the voice becomes resonant and the appetite increases. Also, the yogin whose subtle pathways are thoroughly cleansed is always "full-hearted," energetic, and strong. The Hatha-Yoga-Pradipika mentions leanness and brightness of the body as indications of a purified nadi system. Now the practitioner is like a finely tuned instrument and ready to engage the higher processes of Tantra, leading to the activation of the serpent power.

10.1. AWAKENING THE GODDESS ENERGY

In the human body, which microcosmically replicates all cosmic principles and levels of existence, the divine Energy expresses itself in two principal forms-the life force (prana) and the serpent power (kundalini-shakti). The life force is universally present in the cosmos and as such is known as mukhya-prana or "primary life force." It assumes the following five functional aspects in connection with the human body:

1. prana, in the sense of the ascending vital energy that is chiefly located in the area between the navel and the heart and is linked particularly with inhalation but can stand for both inhalation and exhalation;
2. apana, which is the descending vital energy associated with the the lower half of the trunk and with exhalation;
3. vyana ("through-breath"), which is the vital energy circulating in all the limbs;
4. udana (lit. "up-breath"), which is connection with physiological functions such as speech and eructation, but also the ascent of attention into higher states of consciousness;
5. samana (lit. "mid-breath"), which is localized in the abdominal region where it is connected with the digestive process.

In addition to the above principal types of life force, some scriptures also know of five secondary types (upaprana), namely naga (lit. "serpent"), kurma ("tortoise"), kri-kara ("kri-maker"), deva-datta ("God-given"), and dhanam-jaya ("conquest of wealth"), which are respectively associated with vomiting (or eructation), blinking, hunger (or sneezing), sleep (or yawning), and decomposition of the corpse respectively.

From a yogic perspective, the two most important forms of the vital energy are prana and apana, because they are the subtle realities underlying the flow and the ebb of breathing. Breath control directly impacts on the ascending and descending current of the life force, which naturally alternates-roughly every eighty minutes-between the channel on the left (called ida) and the one on the right (called pingala) of the central pathway.8 The ultimate purpose of breath control is to activate the flow of prana through the central passage, which then draws the much more powerful energy of the kundalini into it.

By means of the kinetic energy of prana, which is freely available in the body and its environment, the yogin can tap into the energetic matrix, the Goddess Power, itself. The psychoenergetic center at the base of the axial channel corresponds to the lowest level of manifestation. It is the terminal point of cosmic evolution, as powered by Shakti. Here the Goddess comes to rest in the earth element. Far from having exhausted itself, this supreme Power now simply exists as sheer potentiality awaiting its reawakening through conscious action. The Sanskrit texts speak of the kundalini as being "coiled up" three and a half times around the linga, the "sign" of Shiva. The coils have been taken to refer to the ground of nature (prakriti) and its three primary constituents or qualities-sattva, rajas, and tamas. This notion may be related to the Vedic teaching of Vishnu's three steps by which he crossed the entire universe. Only a being greater than the universe can traverse it in this manner.

In the case of the serpent power, this transcendence is suggested by the extra half a coil. The name kundalini actually means "she who is coiled" and is related to the word kundala denoting the kind of "earring" worn by some practitioners of Hatha-Yoga, notably members of the Kanphata sect. Some texts shorten the word to kundali, while others use the term kutilangi ("crooked-bodied"). The coils of the kundalini graphically convey the notion of potentiality.

We can understand the evolutionary process from the transcendental plane to the earth realm through an analogous model furnished by modern cosmology. At the "time" of the Big Bang, the world existed in a state of unimaginably condensed ball of energy, sometimes called "quantum vacuum." Suddenly (and for no known reason), some fifteen billion years ago, a chain reaction occurred in this original high-energy soup which led to the creation of hydrogen atoms.

This event coincided with the emergence of space and time and the gradual formation of our spatio-temporal universe, with its billions of galaxies, supernovas, black holes, and quasars, and the cold dark matter interspersed between them. Within this unimaginable vastness are planet Earth and the human species-both products of the original flash from chaos to cosmos or, in Indian terms, of Shiva's ecstatic dance.

Now scientists are busy exploring ways of freeing up the energy stored in matter by smashing high-energy subatomic particles into protons. The yogins are engaged in a parallel operation in the laboratory of their own body-mind. They use the vital energy to repeatedly "smash" against the blocked opening of the central pathway of the nadi system. The Goraksha-Samhita describes this process very clearly:

1. The serpent power, forming an eightfold coil above the "bulb" (kanda), remains there all the while covering with its face the opening of the door to the Absolute.

2. Through that door the safe door to the Absolute can be reached. Covering that door with her face, the great Goddess is asleep [in the ordinary individual].
3. Awakened through buddhi-yoga12 together with [the combined action of] mind and breath, she rises upward through the sushumna like a thread through a needle.
4. Sleeping in the form of a serpent, resembling a resplendent cord, she, when awakened by the Yoga of fire [i.e., mental concentration and breath control], rises upward through the sushumna.
5. Just as one may forcibly open a door with a key, so the yogin should break open the door to liberation by means of the kundalini.

All are agreed, however, that the serpent energy must ascend along the central pathway, which is also called the "great path" (maha-patha) and "cremation ground" (smashana) because it alone leads to liberation. In keeping with this typically Tantric symbolism, the Gheranda-Samhita specifies that the yogin engaged in this esoteric practice should besmear his body with ashes, which is an outward sign of his internal renunciation of all worldly things and desires. The adept who seeks to arouse the kundalini must be prepared to die, because this process quite literally anticipates the death process. As the serpent power rises along the central passage, the yogin's microcosm is gradually dissolved.

A cobra is dangerous only when it is coiled, ready to strike in an instant. However, when its body is completely erect it is quite harmless. Similarly, the kundalini is dangerous only in its form of the diffuse life energies, which fuel the unillumined person's hankering for sensory and sensual experiences, entangling him or her ever more in worldly karmas. When the serpent power is erect, however, it is not poisonous but a source of ambrosia, because it is erect only when it has entered the central pathway leading to liberation and bliss.

The ascent of the Goddess power in the body is associated with the progressive dissolution of the elements-a process that is called laya-krama ("process of dissolution") or laya-yoga ("discipline of dissolution"). In the present context, the technical term laya refers to the resorption of the elements into the pretemporal and prespatial ground of nature (prakriti-pradhana).

In principle, laya is effected as the kundalini rises from center to center. Its arrival causes each center to vibrate intensely and to function fully, but as it goes to the next higher psychoenergetic center, the departure of the Goddess power leaves the previous center or centers as if void. The reason for this is that at each center, Shakti works the miracle of a profound purification of the elements (called tattva), rendering them extremely subtle. More precisely, their vibration is speeded up to the most subtle level of nature (prakriti), and hence they are said to have become reabsorbed into the cosmic matrix. The intelligent Goddess power henceforth-or at least for the period of kundalini arousal-takes over their respective functions.

This esoteric process is the basis for the bhuta-shuddhi ritual in which the elements are visualized as being purified through their progressive absorption into the divine Shakti. This practice is done prior to visualizing oneself as one's chosen deity (ishta-devata) and doing ritual worship. The earth element governs the area between the feet and the thighs; the water element has authority over the area between the thighs and the navel; the fire element rules the zone between the navel and the heart; the air element is reigns over the section between the heart and the forehead; the ether element governs the area above the forehead. The practitioner visualizes earth dissolving into water, water into fire, fire into air, air into ether, and then ether into the higher principles (tattva) until everything is dissolved into the Goddess power itself.

Thus the yogin starts out as an impure being (papa-purusha) and through the power of visualization recreates himself as a pure being, a worthy vessel for the divine Power. Through the kundalini process, this visualized pure body-mind then becomes actuality, for the ascent of the serpent power through the axial pathway of the body recapitulates the mental process of bhuta-shuddhi, literally changing the body's chemistry. Through repeated practice of kundalini-yoga, the Tantric adepts succeed in speeding up the vibration of their body permanently, leading to the creation of the much-desired "divine body" (divya-deha).

Along the route, the ascending kundalini may produce all kinds of physiological and mental phenomena, which are all the result of incomplete identification with the Goddess power and a certain attachment to the body. The Tantras mention startled jumping (udbhava or pluti), trembling (kampana), whirling sensation (ghurni), drowsiness (nidra), as well as ecstatic feelings (ananda) that are not, however, of the same magnitude or significance as the supreme bliss of transcendental realization.

The ascent of the serpent power through the six principal "wheels" of the body is technically called shat-cakra-bhedana or "piercing the six centers." This curious expression is explained by the fact that in the ordinary individual, the cakras are undeveloped and more like knots (granthi) than beautiful lotus flowers. The awakened kundalini breaks them open, disentangles their energies, vitalizes and balances them. Three of the cakras represent a particular challenge to the yogin. Thus the

Tantric and non-Tantric scriptures mention three knots at the base of the spine, the throat, and the "third eye."

The goal of Tantra is to have the kundalini remain permanently elevated to the topmost psychoenergetic center, which state coincides with liberation. At the beginning, however, the kundalini will tend to return to the cakra at the base of the spine, because the body-mind is not yet adequately prepared.

Tantra-Yoga aims at dissolving the illusion of being a separate finite entity, and it does so by means of the union of the kula-kundalini with the transcendental principle of akula, or Shiva. When this is accomplished there is nothing that is not realized as utterly blissful. Even the body, previously experienced as a material lump (pinda), is seen to be supremely conscious and suffused with the nectar of bliss and at one with all other bodies and with the universe itself.

GLOSSARY

Abhyasa: Practice—the act of practicing.

Acharya: Teacher.

Adwaita: A philosophy according to which there is no duality—only a singular state of consciousness.

Agni: Fire.

Agnisar kriya: One of the shatkarmas (cleansing practices)-intestinal cleansing.

Aham: Ego.

Ahimsa: Non-violence, non-injury—one of the yamas of ashtanga yoga.

Ajapa japa: Spontaneous repetition of 'soham' mantra.

Ajna chakra: Energy center located behind the forehead, also called psychic centre—one of the seven energy centers.

Akasha: Ether, space.

Anahata chakra: Energy center located in the heart region; also called pranic centre—fourth of the seven energy centers..

Ananda: Bliss, ecstasy.

Ananda yoga. Gentle, inward yoga that uses silent affirmations while in the asanas (postures).

Antar dhauti: Internal yoga cleansing (shatkarma) techniques.

Antar kumbhaka: Internal breath retention. The stage of pranayama where breath is retained after inhalation.

Antar mouna: Internal silence—a meditation practice.

Antar: Inner, internal.

Anubhava: Experience, realization.

Anusara yoga: Called heart-oriented, this yoga integrates the celebration of the heart, universal principles of alignment, and energetic asanas.

Aparigraha: Nongreed (one of the yamas).

Ardha dhanurasana: Half bow yoga pose.

Ardha matsyendrasana: Half spinal twist yoga position.

Ardha padmasana: Half lotus pose.

Ardha: Half.

Asanas: Yoga postures. Probably the most famous pose is the lotus position, which can really tangle up beginners. Don't do this one without professional help. Pronounced AH-sah-nahs.

Ashram: Retreat or secluded place, usually where the principles of yoga and meditation are taught and practiced.

Ashtanga yoga: The eight fold path of yoga as outlined by Patanjali: Yama, niyama, asana, pranayama, pratyahara, dharana, dhyana, samadhi.

Ashwini mudra: Practice of contracting the anal sphincter.

Asmita: Ego, individuality, I-am-ness.

Asteya: Nonstealing (one of the yamas).

Atman: Soul.

Avidya: Ignorance.

Bahir kumbhaka: External breath retention. The stage of pranayama where breath is retained after exhalation.

Bahir: Outside, external.

Bahiranga trataka: Concentrating the attention (gaze) upon an external object such as a candle flame.

Bandha: A posture in which organs and muscles are contracted to create energy lock in a specific area.

Basti: A colon cleansing technique (shakarma), yogic enema.

Bhagvad Gita: A part of the famous Hindu epic 'Mahabharata'. Teachings of Lord Krishna to his disciple Arjuna at the commencement of the battle of Kurukshetra, with explanations on sannyasa yoga, karma yoga, bhakti yoga, and jnana yoga.

Bhakti: Devotion.

Bhakti yoga: The path of devotion.

Bhastrika pranayama: 'bellows' breathing technique in which the breath is forcibly drawn in and out through the nose in equal proportions, like the pumping action of the bellows.

Bhramari pranayama: Breathing practice in which a soft "humming-bee" sound is produced during exhalation to stimulate the Ajna Chakra.

Bhujangasana: Cobra' pose.

Bikram yoga: A rigorous yoga performed in a hot environment.

Brahmacharya: Purity, chastity, nonlust (one of the yamas).

Brahman: The absolute. Divinity itself, God as creator.

Buddhi: The intellect.

Chakras: Centers of radiating life force or energy that are located between the base of the spinal column and the crown of the head. Sanskrit for "wheels." There are seven chakras that store and release life force (prana).

***Chandra nadi*:** Ida nadi.

***Chandra*:** Moon.

***Chidakasha*:** Psychic space in front of the closed eyes, just behind the forehead.

***Chin mudra*:** Hand gesture in which the first finger is kept at the root of the thumb, the last three fingers are unfolded.

***Danda*:** Stick.

***Danda dhauti*:** One of the cleansing techniques (shatkarmas), used to clean the oesophagus with a stick.

***Dhanurasana*:** Bow' pose; backward bending yoga pose.

***Dharana*:** Practice of concentration; sixth of the eight fold path in ashtanga yoga.

***Dharma*:** Self-discipline, the life of responsibility and right action.

***Dhauti*:** Second of the shatkarmas; cleansing technique of the eyes, ears, tongue, forehead, oesophagus, stomach, rectum and anus.

***Dhyana*:** Meditation; single-pointed focus of mind on either a form, thought or sound.

***Diksha*:** Initiation given by the guru.

***Dosha*:** Three humours of the body—kapha, pitta, vata.

***Dugdha neti*:** Nasal irrigation or cleansing technique using milk.

***Ghrita neti*:** Neti (nasal cleansing technique) performed with ghee.

***Gomukhasana*:** Cow's face' posture.

***Gorakshasana*:** Yogi Gorakhnath's' pose.

Guna: Quality of nature viz. tamas, rajas, sattwa.

Guptasana: The 'secret' pose.

Guru: Spiritually enlightened soul, who can dispel darkness, ignorance and illusion from the mind and enlighten the consciousness of a devotee/disciple.

Hatha yoga: Many yoga styles spring from hatha. It is the yoga of physical well-being, designed to balance body, mind, and spirit.

Hridaya akasha: Psychic space of the heart centre.

Ida nadi: One of the main energy channels running on the left side of the spine from the mooladhara (base) chakra to the ajna chakra in the head.

Integral yoga: This yoga style places almost as much emphasis on pranayama (control of breath) and meditation as it does on postures.

Ishvar-pranidhana: Center on the Divine (one of the niyamas).

Iyengar yoga: This yoga style focuses on the body and how it works. It is noted for attention to detail, precise alignment of postures, and the use of props.

Jala basti: The yoga technique of enema using water—one of the yoga shatkarma.

Jala neti: A shatkarma technique—cleansing of the nasal passages with water by alternating the flow of water in the nostrils, preferably using a neti pot.

Jala: Water.

Jalandhara bandha: Throat lock' to restrict the flow of bereath through the throat—done by resting the chin on the upper sternum (chest).

Japa: Continuous chanting i.e repetition of a mantra.

Jihva dhauti: One of the shatkarma techniques for cleansing the tongue.

Jnana mudra: The gesture of knowledge—in this the index finger is bent so that its tip is joined with the tip of the thumb, the other three fingers are spread out.

Jnana yoga. The path of knowledge or wisdom.

Jnana: Knowledge, understanding, wisdom.

Kapal: Skull or cerebrum.

Kapalbhati pranayama: A breathing technique aimed at cleaning the frontal part of the brain; also called skull polishing—done through rapid breaths with more force on exhalation.

Karma yoga: The yoga of action—aims at supreme consciousness through action; discussed in Bhagavad Gita.

Karma: Action; the act of doing.

Karna dhauti: One of the shatkarma which involves cleansing the ears.

Kati chakrasana: Waist rotating' pose..

Kevala kumbhaka: Spontaneous cessation of breath without any conscious effort.

Klesha: Afflictions or tensions—according to yoga there are 5 such afflictions present in humans from birth.

Koormasana: Tortoise' pose—an advanced posture.

Kosha: Sheath or body; realm of experience and existence.

Kripalu yoga. This yoga style emphasizes proper breath, alignment, coordinating breath and movement, and "honoring the wisdom of the body."

Kriya: Activity, dynamic yogic practice.

Kriya yoga: the practice of kundalini yoga.

Kukkutasana: Cockerel' pose.

Kumbhaka: Breath retention.

***Kundalini shakti*:** Refers to the human's potential energy lying dormant in mooladhara (base) chakra like a coiled serpent. When awakened it rises up through the sushumna nadi.

***Kundalini yoga*:** Philosophy expounding the awakening of potential energy and inherent consciousness within the human body and mind.

***Kundalini*:** Man's retained energy or potential energy and consciousness.

***Kunjal kriya*:** A shatkarma (cleansing) technique that involves the cleansing of the stomach by drinking in water and then expelling it by inducing vomiting.

***Laghoo shankhaprakshalana*:** A shatkarma technique—also referred as the short intestinal wash. Involves the drinking of several glasses of water and the expelling it through stool after a series of exercises (asanas); in the process a thorough cleansing of the colon takes place.

***Laya yoga*:** Union with the supreme consciousness through pranayama or devotion. Literally, union by absorption.

***Maha*:** Great.

***Maha bandha*:** The great lock—combines the three locks in yoga—the moola bandha, jalandhara bandha and uddiyana bandha—together with breath retention.

***Maha mudra*:** The great gesture—combines the practice of moola bandha, shambhavi and khechari mudras simultaneously.

***Maha nadi*:** Literally means 'great nadi', which is the 'sushumna' in yoga.

***Makara*:** Crocodile.

***Makarasana*:** Crocodile' pose.

Manas chakra: The energy center above the ajna chakra—is depicted with six petals.

Mandala: A circular geometric design that represents the cosmos and the spirit's journey. It is a tool in the pilgrimage to enlightenment. One of the most famous mandalas appears on the floor of the Chartres Cathedral in France. It is not uncommon for churches in the United States to recreate well-known mandalas and call them labyrinths. Spiritual pilgrims literally walk the labyrinth to attain spiritual insight.

Manipura chakra: The energy centre in the spinal column located behind the navel—corresponding to the solar plexus.

Mantra: Subtle sound vibration, which through repetition aims at expanding one's awareness or consciousness.

Mantra shakti: The power of mantra.

Matsyendrasana: A spine twisting pose.

Mayur: Peacock.

Mayurasana: Peacock' pose—advanced pose aims at strengthening the arms and stimulating the manipura chakra.

Meditation: Technique of inward attention. Psychologist Lawrence LeShan offers a down-to-earth definition: The goal of meditation is "to enable you to get more out of life and to move more completely in whatever directions you choose." Those directions can range from moving toward inner peace and higher spirituality to losing five pounds before Christmas.

Moksha: Liberation from the cycle of birth and death.

Moola bandha: Energy lock created by the contraction of the perineum in the male and the cervix in the female.

Moola: Root.

***Mooladhara chakra*:** Lowest energy centre in the human body where the kundalini shakti (serpent power) resides—situated in the perineal floor in men and the cervix in women.

***Moorchha pranayama*:** Fainting or swooning breath' in which the breath is inhaled slowly and retained for an extended period.

***Mouna*:** Silence—the practice of silence.

***Mudra*:** Literally means 'gesture'—mudra expresses and channelizes cosmic energy within the mind and body.

***Nadi*:** Energy channels in the body, similar to the meridians in acupuncture.

***Nadi shodhana pranayama*:** Breathing technique—is the 'alternate nostril breathing' or 'balanced breathing'—balances the energy flow in the channels and purifies the energy channels (nadi) by balancing the flow of breath through the right and left nostrils.

***Namaste*:** This Hindu salutation says "the divine in me honors the divine in you." The expression is used on meeting or parting and usually is accompanied by the gesture of holding the palms together in front of the bosom.

***Nasagra/nasikagra mudra*:** Hand gesture adopted during pranayama to alternate the flow of breath through the nostrils.

***Nauli*:** Abdominal massage'—a cleansing technique (shatkarma) involving the contraction of the rectus abdominal muscles.

***Neti-neti*:** Means "Not this. Not this." In meditation, you gently dismiss thoughts, images, concepts, sounds, and distractions by applying the principle of neti-neti or telling yourself, "Not this. Not this."

Neti kriya: Another shatkarma (cleansing technique)—involves cleaning of the nasal passages or; jala neti forms a part of the various neti kriyas.

Nidra: Sleep.

Niyamas: In the *Yoga Sutras,* Patanjali defined five niyamas or observances relating to inner discipline and responsibility. They are purity, contentment, self-discipline, study of the sacred text, and living with the awareness of God.

Om or Aum: Mantric word chanted in meditation. Paramahansa Yogananda called it "the vibration of the Cosmic Motor." This one word is interpreted as having three sounds representing creation, preservation, and destruction.

Pada: Foot; section of a literary work.

Padmasana: Lotus pose—a seated meditative posture.

Pancha makara: The five tantric practices : Mansa(meat), madhya(wine), matsya(fish), mudra(grain), and maithuna(sexual intercourse).

Pancha tattwa: The five elements—earth, water, fire, air and ether.

Param: Highest, supreme, God.

Paramatma: The supreme atma; God.

Parichaya avastha: Stage of perception of nada.

Paschimottanasana: Back stretching pose.

Patanjali: Author of the Yoga Sutras and preacher of the eight-fold (ashtanga) yoga.

Payaswini nadi: Energy channel terminating at the right big toe, between poosha and pingala channels.

Pingala nadi: One of the main energy channels running on the right side of the spine from the mooladhara (base) chakra to the ajna chakra in the head by intersecting various chakras on the way.

Plavini pranayama: Breathing technique which involves gulping air and swallowing it into the stomach and retaining it.

Poornima: Full moon night.

Prakamya: Fulfillment of desire.

Prakasha: Inner light.

Prakriti: Nature.

Pramana: Proof.

Prana: Vital energy force sustaining life and creation.

Pranayama: Method of controlling prana or life force through the regulation of breathing.

Prasad: An offering usually food to and from the guru or higher power.

Pratyahara: Withdrawing the senses in order to still the mind as in meditation.

Pravritti: Nature of the mind.

Prithvi tattwa: The earth element.

Purana: Eighteen ancient books consisting of legends and mythological narrations dealing with creation, recreation and the genealogies of sages and rulers.

Purusha: Man; pure consciousness.

Purushartha: Purpose of the consciousness, of man's existence- the four basic needs or desires, arth, kaama, dharma, moksha.

Raja yoga: The path of physical and mental control.

Rakta bindu: Red bindu, same as beeja(seed) bindu, shakti bindu; the potentially creative bindu from which creation springs; often refers to the ovum.

Rechaka: Exhalation.

Rudra: Lord Shiva ; Rudra is said to have sprung from Brahma's forehead and is one of the holy trinity.

Sahasrara chakra: Highest energy centre located at the crown of the head.

Sakshi: Witness.

Samadhi: State of absolute bliss, superconsciousness. Yogananda called this the "state of God-union."

Samskara: Impressions stored in the mind that form the basis of our beliefs, attitudes and personality.

Sankalpa: Spiritual resolve.

Sannyasi: One who has renounced the world in seek of self-realization.

Santosha: Contentment.

Sarvangasana: Shoulderstand—an inverted posture.

Sat: Truth.

Satguru: Guru who has attained self-realization.

Sattwa guna: Quality unwavering purity.

Satya: Truthfulness and honesty (one of the yamas).

Seetkari pranayama: Breathing technique which involves hissing leading to a cooling effect upon the whole body.

Shabda Brahman: Cosmic causal state.

Shakti: Vital force; energy.

Shambhavi mudra: A yoga gesture in which one focusses at the mid-eyebrow centre.

Shashankasana: Moon pose.

Shatkarma: The six yogic techniques of purification of the body, viz. neti, dhauti, nauli, basti, trataka, kapalbhati.

Shauca: Purity, inner and outer cleanliness (one of the niyamas).

Sheetali pranayama: Cooling breath'—a pranayama technique that lowers the body temperature by inhaling through the mouth while letting the breath flow in over the tongue.

Shishya: Disciple; student.

Shodhana: Yogic cleansing ritual.

Siddha yoni asana: The female counterpart of the siddhasana meditative posture, in which the left heel presses the entrance to the vagina.

Siddhasana: A meditative seating posture in which the left heel presses the perineum (stimulating the mooladhara chakra); also called as the adept's pose or the 'pose of perfection'.

Sirshasana: Inverted pose—the 'headstand' in which the body is inverted and balanced on the crown of the head.

Sivananda yoga: Relaxed and gentle yoga that encourages a healthy lifestyle: Proper exercise, proper breathing, proper relaxation, proper diet, and positive thinking with meditation.

Soham: Represents a mantra in meditation; literally means, 'I am That'. Represents the Psychic sound with the sound 'so' during inhalation and 'ham' during exhalation.

Soma chakra: Sixteen petalled chakra situated above ajna and manas chakras.

Sukhasana: A comfortable meditative pose; also called the 'easy pose' or simply the cross-legged pose.

Surya bheda pranayama: Breathing technique in which inhalation is done through the right nostril ; increases vitality.

Sushumna nadi: Main energy channel in yoga, in the centre of the spinal cord through which kundalini shakti flows.

Sutra neti: Yogic technique to cleanse the nasal passage using a special thread.

Svadhyaya: Self-study. The process of inquiring into your own nature, the nature of your beliefs, and the nature of the world's spiritual journey (one of the niyamas).

Swadhisthana chakra: Second chakra in the spinal column, above the mooladhara.

Swami: Title of respect for a spiritual master.

Swastikasana: Auspicious pose -meditative posture similar to siddhasana.

Tadasana: Palm tree pose- standing posture.

Tamas: The quality of inertia, laziness, procrastination.

Tantra yoga: This yoga uses visualization, chanting, asana, and strong breathing practices to tap highly charged kundalini energy in the body.

Tapas: Self-discipline or austerity (one of the niyamas).

Tiryaka bhujangasana: Twisting cobra pose.

Tiryaka tadasana: Swaying palm tree pose.

Trataka: One of the cleansing techniques (shatkarma) in which the gaze is focussed upon an object such as a candle flame.

Uddiyana bandha: Abdominal retraction lock'; drawing in of the abdomen towards the backbone after exhaling.

Ujjayi: Breathing exercise that produces sound in the throat with the inhalation. Pronounced you-jie-ah.

Ujjayi pranayama: A kind of breathing technique which produces a light sonorous sound.

Utkatasana: Squatting position .

Uttankoormasana: Tortoise pose.

Vajrasana: The 'thunderbolt' pose; a kneeling posture with buttocks resting upon the heels.

***Vama swara*:** Flow of breath in the left nostril.

***Varisara dhauti*:** Yogic cleansing technique in which a large quantity of water is drunk in conjunction with asanas to cleanse the entire digestive tract; also known as shankhaprakshalana.

***Vashitva*:** Ability to control all objects, living and non-living.

***Vastra dhauti*:** Yogic detoxification technique in which a specially prepared cloth is swallowed and removed after ten minutes, in order to remove mucus from the stomach.

***Vayu tattwa*:** Air element.

***Vedas*:** Four ancient texts- Rig, Yajur, Sama, Atharva, which are further divided into Samhita, Brahmana, Aranayaka and Upanishads. They were revealed to the sages and saints of India which explain and regulate every aspect of life from supreme reality to worldly affairs. The oldest books in the library of mankind.

***Veerasana*:** Hero,s pose—for concentration and discrminative thinking.

***Viniyoga*:** A gentle form of flow yoga in which poses and flows are chosen to suit the student's abilities.

***Vinyasa*:** Steady flow of connected yoga postures linked with breath work in a continuous movement. For example: Sun salutation.

***Vishuddhi chakra*:** One of the energy centres located in the spine behind the throat and connected with the cervical plexus, tonsils and thyroid gland.

***Yamas*:** In the *Yoga Sutras,* Patanjali defined five yamas or ways to relate to others — moral conduct. They are nonviolence; truth and honesty; nonstealing; moderation; and nonpossessiveness.

***Yamuna river*:** Emanating from Yamnotri in the Himalayas and joining Ganga near Allahabd, North India;refers to pingala nadi in the pranic body.

Yoga: Derived from the Sanskrit word for "yoke" or "join together." Essentially, it means union. It is the science of uniting the individual soul with the cosmic spirit through physical disciplines (postures) and mental disciplines (meditation). Patanjali offers the best definition: "Yoga is the cessation of mind."

***Yoga abhyasa*:** Practice of yoga.

***Yoga nidra*:** A deep relaxation technique also called 'yogic sleep' in which mind and body is at complete rest but with complete awareness.

***Yogi*:** Someone who practices yoga. (A female yoga is called a yogini.)

SUGGESTED READINGS

Iyengar, B. K. S., *Light on Yoga,* New York, New York: Schocken Books, 1970, 342 pages.

______________, *Light on Pranayama.* New York, New York: The Crossroad Publishing Company, 1981, 294 pages.

Khalsa, M. S. S. Gurucharan Singh, ed., *Kundalini Yoga/Sadhana Guidelines.* Claremont, CA: Kundalini Research Institute, 1976, 107 pages.

Mumford, Jonn, *A Chakra and Kundalini Workbook.* St. Paul: Llewellyn Publications, 1994, 256 pages.

Narayanananda, Swami, *The Primal Power in Man or the Kundalini Shakti,* Nineth ed. Gylling, Denmark: N. U. Yoga Trust and Ashrama, 1979, 230 pages.

______________, *The Secrets of Prana, Pranayma and Yoga-Asanas.* Nineth ed. Gylling, Denmark: N. U. Yoga Trust and Ashrama, 1979, 230 pages.

Radha, Swami Sivananda, *Kundalini Yoga for the West.* Boulder, CO: Shambala Publications, Inc., 1981, 357 pages.

Saraswati, Swami Satyananda, *Kundalini Tantra.* Munger, Bihar: Bihar School of Yoga, 1984, 486 pages.

Yu, Lu K'uan, *Taoist Yoga,* First American ed. York Beach, Maine: Weiser, 1973, 206 pages.

Vivekananda, Swami, *The Yogas and Other Works,* New York: Ramakrishna-Vivekananda Center, 1984, 974 pages.